In praise of **Get Your Peas in a Row**

"If you are a 6 or 7 figure business owner re
& managing a team that saves you tin
It's a vault of Annabelle's knowledge after con.
companies for the past 20 years. She is THE team-building
and your search for help stops here. Read this book and thank you. .

> **– Lauren Gordon**
> CEO of Gordon Business Consulting

"There is so much to learn from this book, and refer back to. The experience of Annabelle Beckwith is diverse and priceless. This is definitely a MUST read."

> **– Ann Collins**
> Author of *Hope Loss enCourage*

"Leaders will instantly recognise themselves and their businesses in this excellent practical guide to best practice in scaling up for business transformation and growth. Annabelle's range of experience, expertise and distinctive style leaps from every page. The book's founding principles of pragmatic applicability will resonate with leaders in spotlighting growth blockers and seeing how to lay those essential foundations for future success. An important contribution to the genre and not to be missed."

> **– Dr. Lesley Crane** PhD, MA, BSc Hons
> Director of Knowing How

"I loved the way Annabelle Beckwith packed up such simple and yet relevant principles for you to grow your business. Search no more: this book is a roadmap to success."

> **– Danielle Martins**
> Speaker and Co-Author of the Best-Selling book *Rising Up From Mental Slavery: How to Unleash Your Infinite Potential*

"Annabelle has captured a lifetime's learning in this book, boiling down the results into five key factors. I would urge anyone with a desire to propel their business forward to devour the contents of this book and adopt the advice presented within."

> **– Russell Dalgleish**
> serial entrepreneur and Chairman of Scottish Business Network

"Annabelle's book will make you better prepared for the journey of growth, scale-up and change. She offers practical guidance and ideas, delivered in a common sense, no-nonsense approach, which is really refreshing. I recommend this book to anyone looking to achieve their ambition for success and growth."

– Gavin Tweedie
Startup Specialist and CEO of Global Surface Intelligence

"Annabelle Beckwith is an author who hones in on strategic business principles that embody leadership. Her book, **Get Your Peas in a Row**, is a great refresher for any business owner to ensure that their expertise becomes a reflection of paradigms that light up your soul. A must read."

– Pashmina P.
International Best-Selling Author of *The Cappuccino Chronicles Trilogy* and *What is a Gupsey?*

"**Get Your Peas in a Row** is definitely a book that will touch people on a global scale. Annabelle's sharp wit and precise understanding of entrepreneurship, and what is needed to succeed, will absolutely inspire you. A highly recommended read that is sure to create a shift in your business paradigms."

– Judy O'Beirn
International Best-Selling Author of *Unwavering Strength* Series, Founder and President, Hasmark Publishing International

"If the thought of growing your business is intimidating to you, read **Get Your Peas in a Row**. Annabelle details a simple and efficient approach to successfully growing a business, by revealing the '5 Ps' (Personal, Purpose, People, Process and Paradigms). Based on the author's extensive and varied professional experiences, Annabelle's book takes the business owner on a journey that is bound for success!"

– Gisele Maxwell
Best-Selling Author of *Free and Wealthy Beyond Rich*

GET YOUR PEAS IN A ROW

5 key factors
to propel your business forward

ANNABELLE BECKWITH

Hasmark
PUBLISHING
INTERNATIONAL

Editor: Gary Hoffman
gary.hoffman@live.com

Cover & Book Design: Anne Karklins
anne@hasmarkpublishing.com

Cover photograph: Iain Forrest Photography

ISBN 13: 978-1-989756-36-2
ISBN 10: 1989756360

For India and Gregor.
Always and forever my reason 'why.'

CONTENTS

ACKNOWLEDGEMENTS

I would like to thank the following people who have been of huge help to me in the writing of this book, and without whom it probably would never have been completed:

My mum and dad and my children, for listening to me talk about the book incessantly for months, and for their constant encouragement.

Ian Thomson and John Moore, for their valuable feedback and insights.

Liz Dexter, my long-time friend and editor.

My friends and colleagues at Hemsley Fraser.

Kirsty Innes and Susan Grandfield, who have been a big part of the journey that has led to this book.

Dr Lesley Crane, for being an amazing role model of leadership in the very earliest days of my career and in the many years since.

And to all my wonderful clients over the years, I owe a debt of gratitude to you all.

INTRODUCTION

"The thing is", he said conspiratorially, "my department is... rather special."

He sat back, smiling, clearly expecting a reaction.

I furrowed my brow. "I see", I said, meeting his gaze and nodding sagely.

What was actually going through my head was, "Funny that – everyone else has said exactly the same thing."

I'd started working as Commercialisation Manager at a well-known music and drama college a week or so beforehand and I was making a point of going around meeting all the heads of department to discover more about their work, their priorities and how I could help them in this newly created role.

As I had my introductory conversations, a pattern started to emerge. And it was one I'd seen somewhere else just a few months before, when I'd been doing some consultancy work for local government...

There, what I'd seen is that every councillor and civil servant was fiercely protective of their own 'patch'. Staff based in one office in one part of the county were somehow at odds with those based in another office, despite the fact that they were serving the same council and regional community.

They all seemed to believe that they were somehow special and different.

It was a pattern I would see many, many times again over the years, in all parts of the world and in businesses of all sizes and in all sectors: a spurious but wholehearted belief that "we", whether as individuals or as groups, are somehow unique.

Yes, we are.

But also, we're not.

I started to see repeating patterns everywhere: the financial institution going through transformational change – with a charismatic new CEO at the helm – was tussling with the same internal 'human' problems as my elderly mother and her friends volunteering in a local charity shop, who became deeply unsettled when a new area manager wanted to change the style of their window displays.

Similarly, the camaraderie I saw on the rugby field as my young son joined the local club and was 'looked after' by older and more experienced team members wasn't a million miles away from the factory floor of a global drinks producer, where staff approaching retirement would take recent graduates 'under their wing' – as though they saw in them something of their younger selves.

The final piece of the puzzle fell into place for me while I was working on a project for a global bank. I'd been speaking with a man who was the Asia Pacific Regional Director for his section and he was moving to a 'Global Head of' role. He was noticeably apprehensive about this, despite his years of experience in a very senior role.

"No one's ever REALLY ready, though, are they?" he asked, displaying the sort of self-doubt and 'impostor syndrome' that I've seen hundreds of times in my clients, and indeed experienced myself.

"Oh", I thought. "You, too. Everyone, then."

"No", I said. "There's no such thing as 'ready'. We've just got to get on with it anyway."

My own journey, then, hasn't been so much of a bolt-of-lightning, Damascus-like conversion, but more of a gradual realisation of core princi-ples and patterns.

Time and time again I've thought, "Oh – will you look at that. It's happening here, too." And it's happening in so many different businesses and sectors around the world that it can't NOT be true.

We're human beings, basically, and we tend to work on the same general operating system.

We react and respond in fairly predictable ways. Certain approaches work whilst others don't...and still others are downright damaging.

And this realisation, friends, has led to the themes of this book: 5 key areas – The 5 Peas Framework ™ – taken from patterns I've observed and experienced since the early 1990s. I've distilled them into a framework that will help you to grow your business by standing back a little and working with core principles that must be in place in order for you and your business to grow and thrive.

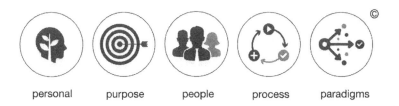

personal   purpose   people   process   paradigms

Personal: Our first focus is on you as an individual business leader (and indeed a human being first and foremost) and on your personal aspirations and capabilities.

Through our explorations of clarity, courage, capability and character, we leverage unrecognised strengths and address development areas: what skills and resources do you already have that you can leverage? What do you need to learn? And what must you now leave behind because it no longer serves you?

Purpose: Unless a business has a clear vision, purpose and goals, it's heading off into the fog without a map.

And of course the secret – the one that no one talks about – is that having these things in place in some abstract way isn't enough. It's how you communicate them and convert them into living, breathing elements in the day-to-day life of your business that makes the real difference.

We'll look at defining your business purpose, direction and strategy, and how to communicate these across functions in a way that everyone can understand, buy into, and put into action.

People: Whatever your current business structure, roles and responsibilities, if you're going through a period of growth, they will need to be reviewed to ensure that they are as future-proof as possible.

Our focus isn't just on what your business needs now; it's on what you'll need in the future.

It's also on the core skills involved in leading your people and building trust, capability and motivation to deliver on your strategy. Even if you aren't a 'people person', these skills and techniques will be vital in bringing your team along with you on your journey.

Process: Your processes and systems, and the extent to which they actively support your people to deliver your strategy, are also crucial. Without them, no business is scalable.

But there's a people side to process that's often forgotten: your team must understand the 'why' behind your processes and own them in order to be able to follow them fully and take accountability for continuous improvement.

We'll look at aligning your procedures and systems for efficiency, AND ensuring that the vital connection between your process and your people is sustained as they move towards your goals.

Paradigms: We've all heard it – culture eats strategy for breakfast. And so it does.

The myth is that culture is an intangible thing that's impossible to manage. There is much talk about how important it is to manage it, but little information as to how.

Whilst it can be a challenge to define and develop, there ARE practical things that leaders can do in order to ensure a positive, healthy and productive culture that can actually make a difference to your bottom line.

We'll look at putting these factors in place in your business.

The long and short of all of it is this: as your business grows, it's going to get messier until it reaches a point where you can't control it instinctively anymore. You'll HAVE to have certain things in place, or it will implode.

It's taken me nearly twenty years to work all this out.

This book will save you having to do the same.

How to get the most from *Get Your Peas In A Row*

Whilst the 5 Peas as principles look as though they can all stand alone, there's a reason for them being in the order I've presented here: one very much leads on from another, and everything is connected.

If you find that things have evolved in a different order by accident, you may well encounter some challenges and need to go back to check that these building blocks are all in place. If you've got a problem with your culture, look to your processes, your team's behaviour, your strategy, and the way in which they are being led by you and your leadership team. If there's an issue with your processes, check to make sure that your people understand what the processes are there to do, and that it's clear how they contribute to your overall purpose and strategy.

The starting point for all of it is you as a person – you as a human being, and not a business leader.

If you don't have a clear idea of what you want in life, there's a risk that you could end up building a business that sucks the life out of you rather than creating one that fulfils and sustains you.

Even if you're thinking, "Let's see how far this thing goes, shall we?!" it's important that you have a clear idea of what you want your life to look like, not just when you 'arrive', but as you journey there.

Once you have this (and a few other things) straight in your mind, you can review your business purpose and overall goals to ensure that they line up. Then from your business goals will come your structure and people, your processes and the paradigms (or culture) that you want to create.

Everything interconnects, but unless ALL the foundations are in place, the thing you build won't be as stable as it needs to be in the long term. You'll find yourself encountering unnecessary problems, and needing to stop and bail out water or fill in gaps rather than focusing on business growth.

That's not to say that you won't encounter any problems if you follow my advice, obviously... you'll just be better equipped to deal with them, personally and practically.

Rome wasn't built in a day, so...

Don't rush through the book. Well, by all means binge-read the whole thing if you must, but come back to the beginning and work through it piece by piece. Spend some time on the activities and considering the questions – these are where the rubber hits the road and where you'll be able to apply these principles to your own life and business.

What you'll find is that you'll already have some of the Peas in place and working well. There will be some that are more or less in place, and there will be some that you didn't even know you needed to have in place.

All of the above are OK: we're all works in progress and we're all constantly learning (or at least we should be) so the fact that there are things that you've not come across yet is part of life. We're all in the same boat here, so never feel contrite at not knowing something. By the same token, don't allow yourself to feel too smug if you do!

Don't rush it – take the time that you need to read, absorb and apply, and (you'll see me say this a lot in the coming chapters) involve your leadership team if you have one, and in some cases, your broader team of employees. Business growth isn't something you can do alone.

Remember throughout to focus on yourself as a person, as well as on your business. We're not just working on scale-up and growth here; we're working on you as a leader and as a person first and foremost.

As the founder, CEO or business leader, this is all very much about you as an individual, your team as individuals, and how you work together to achieve a common purpose.

PEA #1

PERSONAL

*"It is our choices, Harry, that show what we truly are,
far more than our abilities."*

JK Rowling – *Harry Potter and the Chamber of Secrets*

CHAPTER 1

IT'S TIME TO START DEFINING CLARITY

My work with entrepreneurs, business owners and leadership teams always begins with them as human beings – because it has to. The inner work always, *always* comes first, and whilst this book is about business, it's also about life. And it's absolutely about you.

You, the human being, as well as you the business leader.

One of the things that happens in every single coaching group or training programme that I run is that, at some point in the proceedings, delegates breathe a sigh of relief as they realise that everyone in the group is facing similar challenges and issues. Sure enough, the context might be very different – different sectors, different levels of leadership, different sizes of business – but at one level or another everyone is experiencing the same sort of thing.

At the risk of stating the obvious, that's because we're human; whatever the specifics of our situation, we have a finite range of emotions and feelings that we can experience.

We all have, by and large, the same operating system, which is why people all tend to react to change in a similar way, whether it's that major restructure at a global brand, or my mum and her friends volunteering in a local charity shop and dealing with a new manager with new ideas.

Whether that's someone feeling crestfallen at missing out on a life-changing promotion, or the gut-wrenching disappointment my son felt at not being voted Cub Scout of the Year at 9 years old.

Or the joy that an Olympic athlete might feel in winning a gold medal, and the bursting pride I felt in winning the Mums' Race (two years in a row!) at my children's primary school sports day; especially as my daughter's words of encouragement at the start of the race had been, "Don't worry, Mum – it's not the winning, it's the not coming last."

Recognising and understanding our common humanity has a profound impact in two key areas: our understanding of ourselves and our approach to life, and our understanding of those around us – our team, our peers, our colleagues, our employees. At the heart of this lies our understanding of ourselves.

People are at the heart of every aspect of business, even those where this seems to be far from the case. Processes require people to understand, follow and improve them. Automated marketing requires someone to oversee the system to ensure that it's still relevant to customers. We're all doing something created by someone, or working with someone, or working for someone.

At the centre of it all, whoever you are, is you. Which is why we start here. With you.

For any leader looking to grow and scale their business, self-awareness and personal development are crucial. Put simply – your business won't grow unless you do.

This is why our first Pea focuses on YOU and on four key factors – Clarity, Courage, Capability and Character.

Why these four?

Well, if you don't have some *clarity* around who you are, what you stand for, what you want out of life, and where you're going, you could end up in all sorts of trouble. If you don't have the *courage* to take risks and to make bold decisions, your business will crash on the rocks of missed opportunities. If you don't build your *capabilities* as a leader, neither will anyone else, and your business will stagnate. If you're not thinking about your leadership *character* and 'brand', you'll not be building the personal legacy you deserve.

As we shall see in the coming chapters, as the founder/entrepreneur or a key figure within your business, your own personality plays a significant role in shaping the business and its culture, probably in more ways than you realise.

Your Clarity

The pursuit of clarity has to be our starting point. Without clarity, we're all stumbling in the dark. How clear are you, really, on who you are, where you want to go, and what you're doing, in a personal sense? Your business goals and your life goals may be linked...but look at them closely and you'll probably see that they are not the same thing.

For now, I'd like you to focus on your personal goals – whether or not they relate to your business.

The reason for doing so is this: if you are clear about how you want to live your life, you'll be better able to design and build a business that meets those goals, now and in the future. It's also important to bear in mind that growing your business isn't a destination, it's a journey, and it's useful to be clear with yourself at the outset as to how you want to travel on that journey.

So... how clear do you need to be, exactly?

As with most things, it's highly subjective and deeply individual.

Some people will want to see the path laid out before them (in which case watch out, because things rarely work out exactly as planned). Others would rather go with the flow, holding a rough idea of where they are going and seeing what opportunities present themselves (in which case, watch out – if you don't know where you're going, you could end up anywhere).

It's a balance. The point of this section is for you to find out what's right for you.

Clarity around who you are

I was once in a personal development workshop as a participant and the facilitator asked us to introduce ourselves. Nothing new there, you may think, except that he asked us, "Who are you, and how do you know?"

Whilst most of us had been ready to trot out the usual, "I'm Annabelle from Glasgow and I'm a consultant" or some such, this really stopped us in our tracks.

Who am I? Who are you? How do we know?

Why should we care, and how is it relevant to growing a business?!

Several reasons. Who you are, how you think and (as a result) what you do shapes your environment, and therefore shapes your business. As my friend and co-facilitator Irene de Bruin at Shell once wisely said, "When challenges come, you revert back to your default self. So you'd better know who that is."

One of the things I've noticed over the last 20 years is that the character of the leader absolutely shapes the character of their business, whether the leader realises it or not. Who the leader is as a human being has a profound and lasting impact.

So... who ARE you? How do you know?

Who are you outside your business, once you peel the labels away?

Who does everyone else think you are?

One of the most powerful personal development programmes I've been on myself involved 48 people from different backgrounds and walks of life coming together to learn and grow (the PSI 7 programme run by PSI Seminars, based in California). There were people eking it out on $25k a year, and there were people whose personal earnings were close to a million per annum, but our job titles and salaries were irrelevant; what we earned and what we owned didn't define who we were. We had to think much more deeply than that.

In addition to how we viewed ourselves, we became deeply aware of our impact on others, and how they see us. Shortly after the PSI 7 programme, I was speaking to a group of young apprentices about business start-ups. I was introduced as an international consultant, trainer and coach, and my host added, "Global companies that you all know pay Annabelle to train their leaders." When it came to question time, however, someone asked, "Are you India Beckwith's mum?" Turns out she followed my daughter on Instagram.

Who I thought I was wasn't who I actually was...to that particular individual.

Who we are is a combination of who we believe ourselves to be, and who (and how) other people see us.

Why? Because whilst self-perception is crucial, the only person that you can't actually see is yourself. If you don't look for feedback, you won't know how others see you – something that, from a leadership perspective, is also vital.

- How do you define yourself? Do you talk about your job role, or the things that you do or have? Or something more personal?
- What does that definition tell you about how you see yourself?
- How do others define you? What patterns do you see?
- What are you not seeing about yourself, that others could tell you?? (Hint – you won't know until you ask.)

Perhaps more to the point as far as we're concerned in this book...who do you want to become? How do you want people to see you as you grow and develop?

Clarity about your personal values

Your personal values will play out in both your life and your business – it's inevitable.

If you look at your business, how you've built it so far and the culture that has developed and grown, you'll see signs of your own values in action: at an early stage at least, the character of a business is absolutely a reflection of that of the founder.

Now, it's tempting to think of our values as noble concepts like integrity and respect...but often what we value or are driven by are deep-seated factors that we might not want to shout about: the desire to win, for example, or the wish for personal recognition might be very much part of who we are. Joy or humour might be considered lightweight or un-businesslike ... but they may be deeply part of us.

This is not a time to place a judgement on what's appropriate and what's not – it's a time to be brutally honest about what drives you as a human being, and where you can already see this playing out in your business.

So what ARE your values? How do they translate into how you act and carry yourself in daily life, within and outside work? How do they impact the decisions you make?

Have a look at the values list and make a note of all those that are important to you. Add some of your own. This list isn't exhaustive: it's to get you thinking. Be honest and don't attach a moral value to the values – they are what they are, and if they are important to you, then you must recognise this, even if privately.

Later on, when we come to clarify what values your business actually stands for, this thinking process will be important.

AUTHENTICITY	WINNING	FUN	COMMUNICATION	*add yours here...*
ACTION	CALMNESS	STATUS	CREATIVITY	
RESPECT	HUMOUR	WISDOM	KINDNESS	
DEDICATION	HARMONY	TRUST	INFLUENCE	
LOYALTY	JUSTICE	LOVE	FAME	
DISCRETION	RECOGNITION	PLEASURE	COMPASSION	
DISCIPLINE	FAITH	DETERMINATION	PROGRESS	
THOROUGHOUNESS	OPTIMISM	ELEGANCE	FAIRNESS	
PLANNING	REALISM	BEAUTY	FLEXIBILITY	
SPONTANEITY	PEACE	RESPONSIBILITY	RESULTS	
BALANCE	CHALLENGE	SAFETY	SECURITY	
AUTHORITY	ADVENTURE	LEARNING	KNOWLEDGE	
GROWTH	SUSTAINABILITY	ETHICS	LEADERSHIP	
DILIGENCE	RISK	MEANING	SERIOUSNESS	

Once you've picked a handful of values, think about them. Which are most important to you? What could you not live without?

Sometimes when I'm delivering a course or seminar and asking people to think about their values, I'm met with some blank stares as delegates are faced with random, abstract words in a matrix like this.

If this is you, then it might help to do what I ask them to do: take a moment to think about someone whom you admire greatly. It might be someone you actually know – a family member or colleague, for example – or it might be a well-known individual, either alive now or from history.

Once you've thought of that person, think of four or five reasons WHY you admire them.

For example, I've always had great respect for Queen Elizabeth I of England. The daughter of Henry VIII, she grew up in turbulent times and faced great personal danger many times over. As monarch, she exercised wisdom, tolerance, bravery and perseverance. These factors are the values that I hold.

Sometimes negative emotions can help to identify what's important to you. A while ago I was at a business conference that, quite frankly, I found deeply boring. We sat in a large circle and no one seemed to say anything until they had spent several minutes considering what the person before them had said. If anything approaching a lively conversation started to develop, someone would bring it to a halt on the basis that there was 'tension in the room'.

There were constant references to how seriously we took our work, how critical we were about our approach, how reflection was crucial, and how we worked with complexity. Eventually, after sitting in a circle in the conference room for most of the day pontificating on these deep and meaningful concepts, we were promised a 'celebration' in the afternoon.

"Woohoo!" I thought. "Crack open the party poppers!"

What actually happened was that we moved from our sitting circle inside to form a standing circle outside, and each person in turn thought-fully told someone else in the circle how much they appreciated them.

Now, I would agree that there are times when taking a serious approach and being critical in our analysis of events are extremely important. Reflecting on past experience in order to learn is also valuable. Things ARE sometimes complicated.

However, my deep unease and frustration at what I saw as a profoundly dull approach highlighted that my own values were completely the opposite to those of the conference organisers.

I value clarity and simplicity, and seek to break down complex things into manageable parts in order to address them piece by piece.

I'm fatigued by constant criticism. I think people need encouragement, too.

Life is serious enough – I aim to bring humour and joy to my work where appropriate.

Reflecting and deep thought are important... but activity and experiential learning are valuable, too. And to my mind, they are more fun.

So consider carefully: what annoys you in other people? Does someone being rude to a waiter or janitor set your teeth on edge? Perhaps respect for everyone regardless of job title is a thing for you. Is someone too quick to leap on the bandwagon and make decisions? Maybe reflection and diligence are part of your personality. Are you impatient with capable individuals who constantly put themselves down? Perhaps courage is one of your values.

Allow yourself the time to explore your personal values. Understanding them will provide a touchstone in the future when faced with difficult decisions and challenges, and will also help to answer a pivotal question as far as your business is concerned: which values do you want to form the basis of your business culture?

Clarity around your purpose

Having a sense of purpose and being purpose-driven is very much a thing of the moment, and it's led some large organisations to make some fairly exaggerated claims about their 'purpose'. They aren't selling burgers and chips, they claim, they're selling 'families getting together'. They aren't selling time-and-money-wasting online gambling platforms – they're selling fun and a community. Right. Whatever.

The key thing about pinning down your own personal purpose is to keep it absolutely real.

One founder I've worked with, grappling with the pressure of having to come up with some lofty, world-saving personal purpose, struggled to articulate his thoughts on the matter. "I left college with no qualifications", he said. "I needed to earn some money and this is all I can do!"

And you can't say fairer than that. At least he's not making a cynical branding manoeuvre to position himself as the 'good guy' fighting for world peace if that's not who he is and what he stands for.

Having said that, having a sense of purpose is important: we all need to know our reason 'why', and if we look closely enough, we'll all see that it goes beyond the survival tactics of merely earning money.

The internal and the external

So what DOES drive you to do what you do? In all probability there will be a range of factors, some internal and some external.

By that, I mean there will be some that are personal to you (the internal purpose) – that maths teacher who told you you'd never amount to anything, the desire to give your family things you didn't have as a child, the indefinable something that's compelling you towards goals just to see if you can achieve them – that sort of thing.

And there will be an external purpose. You're feeding your internal purpose by running this business...but why? Why this and not something else (beyond "It's the only thing I can do" or "There was a gap in the market")?

Think about the internal reasons that are driving you in your business – the factors that are always there, but that you don't necessarily shout from the rooftops.

- What personally motivates you? (If it's money, look beyond that to consider what the money does for you or means for you.)
- What are you best at? What's your zone of genius?
- When and where are you happiest?
- What do you want for yourself?
- What do you want for your family and loved ones?

These might be personal drivers, but there will be factors inherent in your business that provide an external impetus:

- What difference do you want to make to the customers you serve?
- What difference do you want to make in your broader community?
- What difference do you want to make in the world?
- What legacy do you want to leave?

Clarity about what you want

Let's face it: not all of us have a crystal clear vision of what we want out of life. Even if we do, we find that as time goes on, we change our mind. We might get bored and want to 'pivot' to something else. We might have a family and our priorities change. We might decide to abandon the rat race altogether and go and live off the grid in a forest somewhere.

You MUST, though, have some sort of clarity over where you're going as a person first and foremost, or you might find yourself building a business that becomes a prison, rather than one that sustains and fulfils you.

I've seen this many times before: the high hopes and excitement of business start-up give way to disappointment, dismay, and sometimes despair as the business becomes a Frankenstein's monster, running amok and destroying hopes, dreams and finances.

As we shall see when we come to look more closely at your business, having clarity around your strategy, purpose, and direction is a must. But here, we're looking at what you want personally.

Many years ago, I started a business with a friend. In the excitement of those early days, neither of us stopped to ask the other what we actually wanted out of this. We were too busy doing things – painting the office, speaking to clients, running projects...

I had visions of building a business, hiring a team, perhaps expanding nationally. My business partner, though, had very different thoughts. Where I wanted to invest as much money as possible back into the business, she was looking for a lifestyle business to fund her holidays, her new home and so on. As a partnership, it was never going to work.

There were no rights and wrongs about our differing aspirations – they were just different. Before we went into business together, we should have checked that we were both on the same page, but we didn't.

The key question to be asking yourself at this stage is this: what do you want your business to do for you?

If you know the answer to this, you can set about building a business that delivers it.

Clarity around your goals

What are your goals? What do you want out of life, as well as out of your business?

Does this impact how you run your business...or is your business running you?

Think about goals in three categories: probable, ambitious and wild. A probable goal might be something that's not too much of a stretch – retiring on a reasonable pension and being in good enough health to enjoy it, for example.

An ambitious goal might be a bit of a challenge, but still achievable at a stretch – setting up ten additional income streams within the next year, all of which are earning at least £5,000 a month, perhaps.

A wild goal would be something that you hardly dare to speak about it's so bold. You want to be the next Richard Branson or Bill Gates. You want to be bigger than Oprah. Whatever. Just put it out there anyway, even if only to yourself.

Give it some thought. What ARE your short-, mid- and long-term goals, and in which category do they sit – probable, ambitious or wild?

Whether you're a goal planner or an opportunity taker (or a bit of both), it's important to be aiming for something, and that something needs to be about life, not just about business.

Write them out – commit pen to paper and dare to be really ambitious...

	SHORT TERM	MID TERM	LONG TERM
PROBABLE GOALS	Increase income by 10% in the net year	Build pension	Retire at 60 in good health
AMBITIOUS GOALS	Develop three new income streams this year	Build ten income streams within three years	Be earning at least 100k in passive income within five years
WILD GOALS	Become a multiple best-selling author and international speaker and broadcaster	Be a regular guest on Oprah etc	Be a globally recognised expert, and advisor to government, corporations and the rich and famous.

Clarity about life and business balance

For every entrepreneur bragging online about how wonderful life is, there are hundreds of others who have accidentally traded a 9-5 job working for someone else for a 24-7 in their own business, with a partner who "doesn't understand them anymore" and kids they hardly know.

To an extent, we've probably all been there at one stage or another.

The question is... is it worth it? Only you can decide what's an acceptable work/life balance for you, because building a business isn't just about the end results; it's about the journey, and about being clear where your priorities lie.

I've worked with a number of entrepreneurs in the past who came close to losing their partners, their homes or their sanity over their aspirations. One would take his mobile on holiday and answer every call that came in... and was surprised when his wife grabbed it out of his hands and threw it into the sea.

Another took bad advice from an 'advisor' at the bank who clearly had her own agenda, and put his house up as security against a business loan. The business didn't work out and he lost his home...and almost lost his marriage over it.

Yet another struggled with stress-related depression as they battled to build out their business.

It's entirely up to you what you deem acceptable. But setting out some standards at the outset – and holding yourself to account for keeping to them – will help avoid a situation where you suddenly find yourself in a fix without realising quite how you got there.

It'll also help you to prioritise what's important in your life. There is much talk in entrepreneurial circles about what you must sacrifice for your business. I maintain that it's equally important to be clear about what you WON'T sacrifice, and at what point you'll stop and reflect to avoid burning yourself out.

Wherever you are in that journey, it's time to do a little soul-searching, to ensure that you set boundaries and parameters for yourself.

In my Scaling with Leadership programme (based on The 5 Peas Framework™) I ask the leaders I'm working with to take a piece of paper and do the Life Circles exercise (as shown below). First, they draw a rectangle. This rectangle represents their life.

Then I ask them to draw circles within the rectangle, each one representing an aspect of their life and the amount of time they give to it – things like family, social life, exercise – whatever is relevant to them.

I ask them to do this twice: one to represent where they would, ideally, like to be spending their time, and a second one to represent where their time actually currently goes.

Usually there's a difference between the 'ideally' and the 'actually', and being aware of it can help you to make life choices that will ensure that you're building the right business for you... and that you're travelling the journey in a way that works for you.

For example: Derek currently spends most of his time building his property business. He often works late, and is on hand at the weekend to deal with emergencies if they arise. His family, he knows, is pushed into second place, but he sees this very much as an interim measure. In due course, he wants his operational involvement in the business to lessen as he focuses on new projects.

He is aware that he isn't dedicating much time to his own health, and wants to address this.

The thing is... there aren't enough hours in the day.

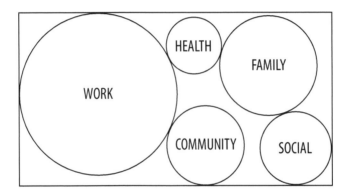

Representing what's going on with the life circles in this simple way can be a real eye-opener. When I first did this, I realised that whilst I was telling myself that my kids were my top priority, I was actually spending far more time at work (and working at home) than I was with them. I allowed work to encroach on time I'd set aside to spend with them, and I didn't hesitate to cut short my time with them if a client needed something.

I justified it by telling myself that, as the breadwinner, I had to be working to bring revenue in; but in truth I'd lost sight of my priorities.

Look closely and honestly at where you're spending your time. Is this how you want it to look forever...or do you need to look at how your business fits into your life, not the other way round?

Give it a go. See what your own life circles look like, and to double check, ask a family member, partner or close friend to give you their perspective.

Clarity about sacrifices

Everyone talks about what entrepreneurs must sacrifice in order to be successful, and they're right.

But as I've already said, YOU decide what to sacrifice – and your family, your sanity and your integrity don't need to be on the list. Nor does sleep or your physical or mental health.

Have a look at your Life Circles and think carefully about what you currently sacrifice for your business.

- What do you want to change? What are you happy with, if it stays the same?

- What's the long-term impact of leaving things as they are?

- What are you prepared to sacrifice/not sacrifice in order to meet your goals and aspirations?

Make a commitment to yourself on the 'balance sheet' below – yes, write it down.

I am prepared to sacrifice		I will NOT sacrifice
	'Audit'	
1.		
2.		
3.		
4.		
5.		
6.		
7.		
8.		

At least monthly, reflect on whether or not you have stuck to this, note it in the 'audit' section, and consider what the impact has been. For example, if you said you'd sacrifice those weekend lie-ins and go to the gym, but in fact you've been lounging around until midday...what then?

If you said you wouldn't sacrifice bedtime stories with your kids, but you've hardly managed to make one bedtime a week, what's the impact there?

There are no rights and wrongs here. It's about finding what works for YOU, in the interests of maintaining your resilience and mental health.

Without these, the game is lost. Or pointless.

CHAPTER SUMMARY

- Be clear about who you are, not just about what you do.
- Know what you want, and why.
- Understand your personal values.
- Know what you want your business to do for you.
- Be clear about what you're prepared to sacrifice, and what you aren't.

NOTES:

_____

_____

_____

_____

_____

_____

_____

_____

_____

_____

_____

_____

_____

_____

_____

_____

_____

_____

_____

_____

_____

_____

_____

CHAPTER 2

COURAGE, MON BRAVE

Leadership requires courage. Heck – LIFE requires courage, and as the old saying goes, courage isn't the absence of fear, it's the ability to move through it.

What IS courage? What does it mean to you? Bravery? Heroism? Standing your ground, holding firm to what you believe in?

Or is it being bold enough to admit you were wrong? To change your mind? To express your humanity and be vulnerable?

What?

What might take a great deal of courage for you – standing up and speaking in public, for example – might be a breeze for someone else. On the other hand, perhaps you're perfectly comfortable explaining the company's financial projections to a potential investor, something that would have others shaking in their boots.

Courage is an individual thing.

Years ago, I was involved in a local authority project to build self-esteem amongst school kids who came from difficult backgrounds. They were seriously troubled in many cases, and the school system wasn't working for them.

We were running a drama project every Wednesday afternoon, encouraging them to step outside the framework of the classroom and learn and work together in a different way. There was one girl who came every week, but stood at the back near the door and didn't take part at all. A traditional 'teacher' approach might have been to insist that she either came and joined in or left, but that wasn't how we were working.

After about six weeks, we had a breakthrough: she took off her coat and came and sat with the others. This might have seemed insignificant to anyone else, but for her, this took extreme courage. She'd taken a big step forward in joining the group rather than continuing to isolate herself.

You'll have experiences like this yourself, or ones that you've seen in other people. Courage is subjective, so there's no need to aspire to the big brave things when the challenge you face is something that means a great deal to you, but might not to anyone else.

At this point, we don't care what anyone else thinks is courageous. We're talking about YOU: you in life, and in general.

Why? Because how we show up in our lives generally is usually reflected in how we show up in our business.

So, what is 'courage' to you? Where do you feel courageous... and where does your courage fail you?

Courage as confidence

Confidence can be elusive. You'll doubtless find that in some situations you feel as though you're on home turf and you function brilliantly. In other situations, self-doubt, impostor syndrome or something else gets the better of you and you feel your confidence falter.

It's important to recognise that situations themselves don't make us confident or fearful; that, friends, is all in our heads. If 'public speaking' was the thing that was frightening, everyone would be frightened by it. The fact that not everyone is indicates that this is about mindset.

It's useful to think about the types of situations (or even individuals) that might cause our confidence to waver. If we can identify these – and it may take a bit of soul-searching to do so, as we'll see – we can recognise what triggers us to falter and address those specific areas.

In which situations do you feel most confident? Think about this as broadly as possible. For example, if your answer is something like "When I'm working with processes and I know what I'm doing", that's great. Expand the context, though. What if you're working with unfamiliar processes and don't quite know what you're doing? What if you know what you're doing, but the process isn't obvious and you're having to make it up a bit? What sort of processes would you be talking about here: technical ones, or behavioural ones? What level of knowledge do you have – a deep understanding or a tenuous grasp?

The point of analysing this is to develop a keener sense of self-awareness: yes, in these situations I am strong. This is my zone of genius. When I am here, I feel secure.

When you are feeling confident, how do you act? What sort of response do you get? You'll probably find that people gravitate towards you, listen to what you say and act on it. They trust you, in other words, and I hardly need say that as a leader in any situation, that's going to be pretty important. If you're not confident, people won't be confident in you, and it will cause them to lose confidence themselves, or to desert you in favour of someone who IS more confident.

If you've not really noticed how people respond to you when you are in 'confident mode', then start to take notice. There will definitely be something noticeable going on, so pay close attention and look for behavioural patterns, in yourself and in your audience. This will provide valuable learning material for your future development – free advice, basically, that's hidden in plain sight, as so many life lessons are.

Having considered what you're like when you're feeling confident (or at the very least, settled), it's important to recognise what happens to you when something or someone shakes that confidence.

What can trigger you to lose confidence? Think carefully here. It may be that you can identify some useful patterns that you can look to address. Are you comfortable in a small group but feel daunted in a crowd? Are you happy when you have to improvise in the moment, but feel under pressure when you have definite instructions to follow, or vice versa? Do you feel your nerves getting the better of you when faced with people in authority or seniority... perhaps one or two individuals in particular?

Often we lose confidence when we compare ourselves to others: "They seem to have it all figured out, and I don't! What's wrong with me?!" Don't fall into this trap. You'll find yourself comparing your own INside with someone else's OUTside, and that's never going to be a fair comparison. This is about you, not about anyone else.

When you feel your confidence deserting you, how do you act and what sort of response do you get?

I was travelling from the UK to the USA via Dublin to attend a training course a year or so ago, and it transpired that the US immigration desks were actually at Dublin airport, saving time once you'd got to the States. I had nothing to hide – I was attending a high-calibre programme in California, my return flights were booked, I had the relevant visa and I'd been clear about the specific address at which I'd be staying.

So when the immigration official asked me where I was going, you'd have thought that I'd be perfectly confident in my response. But I wasn't. I completely forgot the name of the town I was going to, and as I flailed about trying to dredge it from my memory banks, I became aware that I was starting to sound pretty suspicious. Of course, this in turn made me all the more flustered.

Thankfully I can't have come across as a threat to national security because I was allowed to pass and wished a pleasant flight, but the point is this: sometimes even though we're in the right and perfectly confident, something can happen to throw us off course. Someone fixes us with a steely glare and a pointed question (and yes, even the simple, "Where are you going, ma'am?" seemed like an interrogation at that immigration desk). Our thought process veers from normal and rational to "What if I'm wrong? He doesn't believe me! What if he doesn't let me pass? I bet I look like an idiot..." and so on, none of which is helpful.

How you feel physically has a bearing on all this too. You know what I mean – that sudden lurching feeling in your chest or stomach, an embarrassment; a flaring of anger or annoyance perhaps, again often felt in the chest; or maybe a sudden flash of heat in your face. Think carefully – when you start to lose composure, how PHYSICALLY do you feel it?

Does it cause you to lash out? To start babbling like an idiot (like me at the immigration desk)? To shut up completely for fear of making things worse? (All of which usually make things worse, actually.)

Recognising and being aware of the physical signs will enable you to spot them when they flare up in the moment, so you can do something about them. I recommend telling yourself to "Stop. Breathe. Think" in that order. Stop for a moment before your emotions get the better of you. Breathe to get oxygen to the brain and allow yourself a moment of composure, and to focus on the present. Think in a more responsive rather than reactive way.

To reiterate, the most important point of all is to acknowledge that when situations, people, environments, or other factors undermine our confidence, it's our THINKING about these factors that makes all the difference. As Captain Jack Sparrow says in one of the Pirates of the Caribbean films: "The problem isn't the problem. Your attitude to the problem is the problem."

With that in mind, it would be useful to look at a few thinking processes that I often share with my clients. Don't worry, it's not going to turn into an academic dissertation here – I'm all about keeping things practical and applicable.

Courageous thought processes

Courage requires presence of mind, and the ability to respond with presence of mind rather than reacting from a place of emotion.

That phrase, 'presence of mind', is a crucial one here. It's very easy indeed to sink into a state of panic and become overwhelmed at the circumstances in which we find ourselves – we've all been there. Deadlines are looming, the kids have a dental appointment, your spouse has invited the in-laws for supper, and you've got a million and one things marked 'urgent' on your 'to do' list. It only takes one more thing, however small, to send you into a tailspin of despair that you'll never be on top of things again.

And it's a horrible feeling – tightness in the chest, a feeling of nausea, clammy hands...and once we've got to this point, it can be difficult not to lose the plot completely.

Again, a simple phrase to bring to mind and act upon is "Stop. Breathe. Think."

Think about what you're thinking, where it's coming from, and above all, how useful that train of thought actually is. Whether or not it's true is immaterial: the key point is whether or not it's useful and will take you forward, out of the situation.

The 'Behaviour Cycle'

I stumbled on this several years ago and have used it in many training and coaching programmes with clients over the years. Often it's the single biggest thing that they take from the programme. Why? Because they suddenly see their own behavioural patterns, situations and outcomes in a completely different light.

It's a variation on the 'Betari Box', which draws links between our attitudes, our behaviours, and the attitudes and behaviours of others, but it goes a little further.

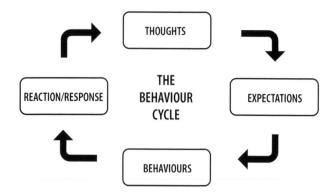

There are numerous variations on this cycle, and you may hear it referred to as the belief cycle. Either way, it points to one key factor: it all starts with what's going on in your head.

In essence, the thoughts (and feelings) that we have will govern our expectations of the situation that we're in or about to go into.

Our expectations will dictate our behaviour, our body language, and other non-verbal behaviour, as well as what we subconsciously do.

Our behaviour will impact the response we get from other people, and the outcome of the situation.

And, of course, it can turn into either a negative or a positive cycle.

Several years ago, I was asked to deliver a workshop on sales presentation skills at a conference for the European and USA teams for a global organisation in the defence industry. For reasons which will become obvious in a minute, I can't say which company it was.

The brief wasn't one to fill my heart with joy. After phone conversations with both the UK Director and the US Vice President of Sales, the following was put to me:

- This was to be a compulsory session, and some of the delegates didn't see why they should attend.

- Some older members of the sales team were using old-fashioned methods that simply weren't as effective any more... but they thought that they were 'experienced' and therefore great.

- Some were hopeless at explaining technical concepts in layperson's terms to their prospective buyers, who might not have had an engineering background.

To add to this less-than-edifying scenario, I was, at that point, a woman in my mid-30s, and the session would be with around 60 men of varying ages, some of whom had been in their roles almost as long as I'd been alive.

To begin with, every time I thought of the forthcoming workshop, I felt physically sick. I imagined a buttock-clenchingly awful scene in which no one was listening to me; I was prancing about like a court jester desperately trying to engage the group, whilst the participants chatted amongst themselves at their tables, or simply got up and left the room.

Thankfully I managed to Stop, Breathe and Think, and, with considerable effort, get a grip. Every time I caught myself thinking, "This is going to be the worst moment of my career", I told myself that I might not be an engineer but I DID know how to present and sell... and that I was going to put on a show and work with the people who wanted to work with me.

I must emphasise that this wasn't a one-off thing –EVERY time I caught myself dreading the prospect of the workshop, I consciously said to myself, "I'm going to put on a show, and work with those who want to work with me."

On the day of the workshop, I arrived at the venue and crept in at the back of the room whilst the previous speaker was finishing. The American VP of Sales came up to me. "You'd better be good!" he said, shaking my hand with a vice-like grip.

Had I persisted in telling myself how dreadful the day was going to be, this remark alone would probably have sent me crying to the toilets.

As it was, I had talked myself up to the point where I smiled politely and said something vague in response... but what I thought was, "It's your lucky day, boyo, because I AM!!"

Had I carried the thought, "This will be awful", my expectations of the day would have been that it was going to be a lot of hard work to no avail, or worse, that it would be a car crash of a workshop where I was a laughing stock and not even my professional reputation could be saved from the wreckage. My body language and approach would have been (subconsciously if nothing else), one of hopeless resignation or desperation. The result would have been pretty lacklustre, I'm sure.

As it was, I was expecting to put on a show and share my expertise. I was expecting most people to be engaged with the session. If they weren't – well, that was their choice. I was expecting the session to go well.

Surprisingly, perhaps, I enjoyed delivering the session, and most of the group came along with me. Sure, there were one or two at the back who weren't taking much notice, but they weren't my focus.

At the end of the workshop, the VP of Sales came up to me and said, "That was great! You didn't just talk the talk, you walked the walk! You really put on a show!" He used the precise phrase that I'd been repeating to myself for the past several weeks.

I'm utterly convinced that my understanding of the behaviour cycle, and the fact that I forced myself to reframe my thoughts, had a profound impact that day.

It gave me courage, where before that, there had been fear (and, not to put too fine a point on it, despair).

Conversely, I can remember hundreds of times where a situation didn't work out to my advantage because of the negative thinking and hesitant self-talk that I was unwittingly carrying with me: "He's a big cheese – he's not going to want to buy my services when company X is in the frame." "All the other conference speakers are respected academics! I'm totally out of my depth here!"And even on a date, "He could choose anybody – why would he see anything in me?"

Be careful what you think, friends. Be very careful indeed.

Take a few minutes to give it some thought and you'll be able to identify situations in your own life where this cycle has very much come into play.

- Where has it worked in your favour... and where has it worked against you?

- How might reframing your thoughts, as I managed to do with some effort at that sales workshop, have brought about a different outcome?

- What thoughts are you currently carrying about your business, your ability to scale up, and your self-perception of you as a leader? If these aren't useful, what will you start telling yourself instead?

These mindset shifts are crucial, not just to life, but to business leadership.

Daniel Ofman's 'Core Qualities'

This is another of my favourite frameworks. When I first came across it, it suddenly shed a light on a number of limiting or unhelpful beliefs that

I'd been carrying with me, especially with regard to leadership and how I related to other people, and indeed about who I wanted to become in the long run.

Daniel Ofman's Core Qualities

There are fuller, more academic explanations, of course, but my interpretation is this:

We all have 'core qualities': traits and behavioural factors that are useful, that people value us for and that have served us well in life.

However, even these positives can sometimes reach a tipping point where they start to work against us. Too much of a good thing can become a pitfall.

Once we recognise this, we can make a conscious choice to accept the challenge of developing ourselves.

However, as we challenge ourselves to develop, our fear of overdoing it can get in the way: we fear becoming the opposite of who we are now, and this is our 'allergy'.

If we don't recognise what's going on, we can shy away from developing our skills in an appropriate way because we fear going too far.

A few years ago I was coaching Tom, who was an expert in international law. He was having issues around his personal impact at work, and this was the focus of our work together.

One of Tom's Core Qualities was that he was a very likeable and popular chap, a friend to most people in the office in which he worked. This, of course, was something he liked and was comfortable with. As our conversations developed, it turned out that he had moved about a great deal as a child, and so had learned how to quickly make friends and 'fit in' at each new school he attended. As a coach, I was more interested in how he was going to move forward than on addressing his past, but his history was very likely to have had a bearing on his current behaviour patterns. It certainly pointed to a 'root fear' of being rejected.

He'd reached a tipping point, though. Too much of a good thing (his Core Quality) was starting to have an adverse effect professionally. His desire to be liked was making him fearful of conflict, and there were times when he simply wasn't being assertive enough when others disagreed with what he was telling them (from a legal standpoint). Professionally, his opinion was valuable, and as the subject-matter expert, he was right in what he was saying, but he lacked the courage to be able to put his message across (especially when it ran the risk of putting him at odds with his colleagues, or saying no to something they wanted to do). Clearly, he wasn't just saying no because he was a pain in the butt, but because there may be serious legal implications if they moved forward with their plans.

His 'Challenge' was to develop his mindset (and a set of behavioural and communication skills) where he both thought and acted more assertively when he needed to, even if it risked a conflict.

His 'Allergy', and the thing that he didn't want to become, was pretty much the opposite of his Core Quality. He was afraid of becoming (or being perceived as) the sort of person who rides roughshod over other people's opinions, or the sort of person who says whatever they like without regard for the impact on others. Ultimately, he feared the rejection to which this might lead.

However, his fear of becoming 'the sort of person who...' was actually holding him back from developing the skills and mindset that he needed.

So how does this relate to you? How does Daniel Ofman's model link to your confidence levels in a given situation? Do you find yourself shrinking away from taking a challenge because, like Tom, you don't want to become 'the sort of person who...'?

I was brought up to be modest about my achievements. I was always told that no one likes a show-off, or someone who's loud and pushy. Over the years, this inhibited me in my learning and personal growth – heck, it even delayed the writing of this book by several years. Why? Well, I didn't want to be seen as someone arrogantly crowing over my own achievements and coming across as though I was totally self-obsessed.

Please don't hold yourself back by making the mistake that I did.

Here's the thing: as I've said before (and will say again), as human beings, whilst we're all unique in ourselves, we work on more or less the same operating system, and we all tend to have similar fears, deep down. Once we move beyond fear of death or injury (the sort of fear that lies behind a fear of heights, for instance), or even an irrational phobia like the fear of birds, they tend to be underpinned by the fear of:

- rejection, abandonment or being alone
- being wrong and being humiliated or shamed
- lack of control

Most other fears are rooted in these.

Think carefully: where do you know, deep down, that you need to develop? What do you fear becoming, that's holding you back?

The 'Ladder of Inference'

Chris Argyris and Peter Senge's 'Ladder of Inference' provides another eye-opener on how our brains work, and it's easy to see how this (like the Behaviour Cycle and Ofman's Core Qualities) can hold us back, or, when we're conscious of it, be leveraged to work to our advantage.

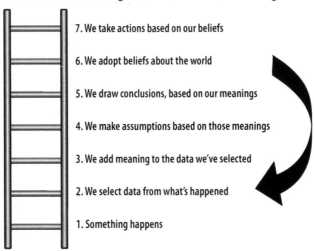

7. We take actions based on our beliefs

6. We adopt beliefs about the world

5. We draw conclusions, based on our meanings

4. We make assumptions based on those meanings

3. We add meaning to the data we've selected

2. We select data from what's happened

1. Something happens

Here's my take on what it all means.

A few years ago I was on a flight from Phoenix, Arizona to Charlotte, North Carolina.

I usually like to sit by the window because I like to look out at the changing landscape, but on this occasion, I'd only managed to get an aisle seat. As we took off, I leaned forward a little and looked out of the window and squinted, as it was very bright outside.

Suddenly, the lady next to me looked at me, then leaned over and snapped the shutter down!

What the?! My immediate reaction was annoyance. What a cheek! What sort of person doesn't want a fellow passenger to look out of the window for goodness sake?!

If I'd been in a REALLY bad mood, I might have thought, "Right, pal – I'm in the aisle seat and I'm going to pretend to be asleep, so if you need to get out to go to the toilet...too bad!"

Here, friends, was the Ladder of Inference in action:

Step 1: Something happens. And that's it. An occurrence takes place (the woman closing the window shutter as I was trying to look out).

Step 2: We select data from the thing that's happened. To be fair, the brain has to filter somehow... and that's exactly what it does.

Step 3: We add meaning to the data we've selected... and here's where it starts to get messy. In my case, it was to think that she'd done something selfish and unreasonable for no reason.

Step 4: We make assumptions, based on the meaning we've added ("What kind of monster ARE you?!").

Step 5: We draw conclusions, based on the assumptions we've made ("You must be one of those people who...").

Step 6: We adopt beliefs about the world ("People like that are always like this" / "People always treat me like...").

Step 7: We take action based on our beliefs ("Right!!! You're not getting out to the toilet!!!").

There are a few key points to make about this. First, it's a cognitive process. It's how the brain works to make sense of the world, and whilst it often doesn't help us, it's something that we all do. And it's not a slow process where we internally say, "Waaaait a minute. What's going on here? Does that mean that...?"

It happens in an instant. We run up that ladder in a fraction of a second, and by the time we get to the top, that is our reality, our truth. We THINK we've made a logical deduction on the basis of the thing that's happened, but we haven't: we're not reacting to the thing, we're reacting to what we think about the thing.

Once we ARE at the top, our helpful brains become trapped in a loop between step 6 and step 2: we start subconsciously selecting data to confirm the beliefs that we've adopted.

You know how it is: if we like someone, they have to do something pretty unacceptable for us to become annoyed. If we DON'T like someone, though, they only have to step a fraction of an inch out of line and we're quick to react: "Look! They're doing it again! I KNEW that would happen!!"

Why? Because we've subconsciously been looking for 'evidence' (ie selecting data) of what we think we already know.

The moral of the story is... don't be too quick to believe what you think.

What if my fellow passenger had simply noticed me squinting out of the window, thought the sun was in my eyes, and so helpfully closed the window so that I wouldn't be blinded? That's actually a far more likely explanation of what happened that day.

Take a moment to look at some of the conflicts that are going on in your life. Where is the ladder in evidence?

How might you 'Stop, Breathe, and Think' in order to question your own thought processes, stop yourself before you react from a place of emotion, and respond with more presence of mind?

Courageous leadership

When we think of 'courageous leadership', it's easy to think of heroic gestures, bold decision-making, leading from the front, inspiring others with grand speeches and so on. And yes, this is often what's involved.

It's important to think about what, for YOU, requires courage, though... and it might be none of the above. As I've already said, courage is not the absence of fear – it's the ability to move past your fear, because move past it you must.

Consider what you shy away from, not just in your leadership role, but in life generally. Where do the core fears that affect us all come into play?

- physical harm
- rejection, abandonment or being alone
- being wrong and being humiliated or shamed
- lack of control

Like many people, I tend to be conflict-averse, and early on in my management career, I really, REALLY hated giving any member of my team negative feedback (call it 'developmental', 'correctional' or what you will... it will always be perceived as negative or critical to the recipient, to start with, at least).

I was worried about upsetting them, worried that they might leave, that they might think I was being heavy-handed or, worse still, make a formal complaint that I was bullying them in some way. All of these stemmed from a root fear of rejection and abandonment by the individual and potentially the wider team.

It took a considerable re-think and learning new techniques for me to start to become more comfortable with having those difficult conversations. For me, courage in that instance involved inner work to get into a mindset where I wasn't catastrophising a conversation in which I was telling a team member to focus more on their targets this next quarter into a ghastly scenario where I was tarred, feathered and drummed out of town.

Think carefully about where you must build courage yourself. You may well find that you've been rationalising why there's no need to do so. Really scrutinise these rationalisations. Are they just excuses?

For some, the ability to admit that they might have been wrong or that they don't have all the answers can require courage, because in their own minds, it puts them in a situation of weakness. For others, it might be a willingness to be vulnerable and open and show up as themselves rather than as the professional business stereotype they think they ought to be.

What is it for you? Bear in mind that the way in which you operate in one area of life is usually very much the way in which you'll operate in another. If you find it difficult to trust people and you don't challenge yourself on this, you'll find it difficult to trust your staff, and this will have implications for your business culture (and ultimately, the execution of your strategy).

If you are conflict-averse generally and you don't address it, it may lead to you failing to take corrective action in your business, which, again, will set up a damaging chain reaction in the longer term.

If you tend to dominate and control in life situations, you'll need to build the courage to let go and trust others to contribute. Don't laugh it off and joke that you're a control freak. Whilst 'leading from the front' might appear to be an advantage, watch out – there are aspects of this approach, if habitually used, that can be deeply damaging for businesses, relationships and your own mental health and well-being.

Think really carefully. It may be easier to avoid having the courage to tackle an issue head on, but what is the long-term impact on you? On those around you? On your business?

Courageous risk-taking and decision-making

Good judgement and decision-making are the hallmarks of a good leader. Such qualities are valuable life skills, anyway. How often has dithering over a decision or making a poor choice set you back in your life and work? It's worth reflecting on some of the decisions you've made over the years to see if any patterns emerge – and to consider whether these have been useful or not.

I don't particularly like shopping for clothes. I'm not one of these people who browses at length through every rail, perusing, selecting and discarding items in a leisurely manner, taking a few to the changing room, asking for the opinion of friends...and then possibly emerging from the shop empty-handed, only to repeat the exercise in every boutique in the street.

No, siree. I go into the shop as if on a military reconnaissance mission, scanning the rails for colours that appeal to me. If something catches my eye, I'll pick it up and consider the cut and shape and the type of fabric. If I REALLY like the look of it at that moment, I'll bother to try it on.

In the changing room, I know as soon as I've put it on whether or not I'm going to buy it. If it feels like I've owned it for years, I'll buy it. If I start to have any doubts whatsoever about the colour, fit, or anything else, I'll put it back, leave the shop, and go somewhere else.

This "scan – select – try–keep or discard –move on" method has shown up elsewhere in my life, too: buying a house, for example. Sometimes it works, and sometimes it doesn't. What I've needed to do over the years is develop the discernment to recognise when a more considered approach is needed. In business, I've made some poor purchasing decisions that could have been avoided if I'd given them more thought.

Conversely, I know people who agonise over decisions, weighing up the pros and cons and gathering more and more data and information, sometimes to the extent that by the time they are ready to decide, the ship has already sailed and they've missed their opportunity.

How do you tend to make decisions?

- Go with your gut.
- Gather all the data and make a considered and informed decision.
- Consider the impact on the people around you before deciding.
- Aim for the long-term, big picture and figure out the details as you go.
- Involve others – they're going to be impacted by the outcome and you want their input early.
- Make them yourself: you alone are accountable for the results.
- Once you make a decision, you stick to it.
- If it looks like you've made a poor decision, you'll change direction.
- You'd rather defer to someone else, to be honest.
- If you're deciding about a new direction, you like to have the confirmation and reassurance of others.
- It depends on the decision – sometimes you'll let others decide, sometimes it's you.
- You're happy to make a big decision but if someone else is pushing forward to do it, you let them get on with it.

There is no right or wrong here; we're talking about you as you are. The key point is to be aware about what your natural tendencies are. Consider where these are useful and work well for you, and where they don't. And, of course, learn to develop the wisdom of knowing which approach to take, and the skills to do so.

It's rarely a case of one-size-fits-all. Whatever your habitual approach to decision-making, there will be alternative perspectives and methods to be learned and added to your portfolio of skills.

One final thing here: do your thinking and evaluating before you make your decision, and once you've made it, move forward. Once you've jumped out of the plane, there's no point worrying about whether the parachute will open – you should have checked that before you took off.

Risk-taking is often a part of making decisions, but the stark fact is that however much information we gather, or however certain we might be of the way forward, we never QUITE know how it's all going to play out. So what's your approach to risk?

- You don't see risk; you only see opportunity. (Aye. Good luck with that.)
- You jump in and then figure it out. Sometimes it works out, sometimes it doesn't.
- You consider every possible risk. Sometimes this stops you from moving forward, or the result is that you lose the advantage of the moment.
- You're mindful of the risks and put plans in place to mitigate against them.

Crucially, how do your current habits impact your life, and how might they be impacting your business?

The courage to grow and change

Growth – whether that's personal growth or business growth – means change. We're all either in a state of growth or a state of degeneration and decay. So, which is it, and what is your personal approach to/response to change?

- You love constant change and get bored without it.
- You're adaptable: when change comes, you're ready.
- Change isn't always good. If it ain't broke, don't fix it.
- You expect others to change to meet your agenda.
- You get annoyed if people expect you to change: "I am who I am."
- When you're ready for change, you expect others to follow.
- You expect people to trust your judgement when you say that change is needed.
- Change means leaving everything behind.
- Change means taking what's valuable with you, and leaving the rest.
- Change is frightening to most people.
- Change is invigorating to most people.

As with risk-taking, decision-making and everything else, our focus here is on your current habits and thinking patterns, and where these might need to be challenged and changed – and how YOU might need to change in order to grow, move forward, and not get stuck in a rut.

As human beings, we tend not to respond to change well. Our brains are hard-wired to keep us safe, comfortable, and among the familiar. The decision to change, break out, grow, build, and do something different is often a bold one.

Take a look at your life and business currently. What's working well, and where are the results in your life not as you might want them to be?

What do you need to change in order to get to where you want to go, and to be who you want to be? By this, I mean what do YOU need to change. It's no good saying, "I need my spouse to become more understanding", or "My team needs to be more productive", or "The government legislation on [whatever] needs to change."

Focus on things within your control, and do the inner work first. You may want different results in your life and business, but the reality is that nothing is going to change unless you do.

Do you have the courage to make those changes? Your future depends on it.

CHAPTER SUMMARY:

- Be aware of situations in which you are naturally comfortable and courageous, and those in which you aren't.
- Consider what (or who) causes you to lose confidence.
- Stop. Breathe. Think.
- Reflect on how cognitive processes are working for and against you.
- Look for patterns in how you deal with decisions, risk and change.

CHAPTER 3:

CAPABILITY
(IT ISN'T JUST WHAT YOU KNOW)

We're starting to focus a little more now on you in relation to your business, although the following concepts are equally applicable in a general life context.

As you grow and build your business, you'll need a fresh set of skills to take you forward. Without a doubt, you'll have to let go of some of the things that have helped you get this far, but which no longer serve you. You'll also have a core set of factors that are working well for you, and which will carry you forward. The trick is to recognise which is which.

I think of this as a choice between 'learn, leverage or leave'.

Let's start by taking a look back at your journey so far, and reflecting on where you've had to 'learn, leverage or leave' attitudes, behaviours and skills as you moved forward. As an aside, I'm relating this (another ladder!) to your business journey, obviously, but you can easily use the same metaphor to reflect on other areas of your life.

The entrepreneurship ladder

Having worked with entrepreneurs and business owners as well as with corporate multinationals over the years, this I know: the learning curve that a business owner goes through as they grow their business isn't a million miles away from the learning curve that a corporate executive goes through as they advance up the promotion ladder.

GROWING ORGANISATION

TEAM 10+

SMALL TEAMS

FIRST HIRE!

SOLO-PRENEUR

Here our focus is on your growing business – but if you've ever worked in a corporate environment, don't forget the lessons you learned there, because they'll be a useful parallel for you here.

Obviously, we start at the bottom of the ladder and work our way up.

Solo-preneur: You're doing everything yourself. You might be outsourcing a little of the really tricky stuff that you don't have a clue about, but by and large you act as chief cook and bottle-washer. You're getting to grips with all the aspects of your business that you hadn't given too much thought to before you started – marketing, IT, finance... the lot.

First Hire: You're stepping into a leadership role for the first time, and you're learning that leading and managing someone else has its own set of skills and challenges.

Small Team: You're building your team, but you're possibly still managing everyone yourself. You may well find that while you're trying desperately to pull yourself away and work ON your business, rather than IN it, you're frequently dragged back into day-to-day operational work or people-related issues.

Team 10+: By this point, you need a leadership team with clear responsibilities and a business structure if you don't already have one. You can no longer directly manage everyone effectively or efficiently, and the structure of your business needs to be designed to make it future-fit.

Growing Organisation: As your business grows, you're moving into an increasingly strategic role, leading the leaders further down your business who are responsible for the day-to-day delivery of results. You have a clear organisational structure in place, and goals, roles and responsibilities are clear. You can focus on your CEO role in driving your business forward.

So, where are you on the ladder? Needless to say, there are skills to be learned at each level, some of which are obvious to you as soon as you get there, and some of which aren't.

Once again, reflecting back on your journey so far is a useful starting point as you focus on moving forward. What patterns of behaviour have marked your journey? What have you forgotten about that actually had a surprising impact along the way? Where did you get in your own way? Where did you take a courageous leap forward, and it paid off?

Learn, leverage or leave?

Think about each stage of the journey, and what you had to learn – in fact, not only that, but what that learning journey was like. The way in which you identified any gaps in your knowledge and set about addressing them is likely to play an important part in your ongoing learning as a leader. Did you decide to learn how to do things yourself, or did you choose to bring in someone else with strengths in your area of weakness, so you could focus on something else?

If you were someone who realised that there was something to be learned but decided just to guess your way through it, ask a couple of pals, or download some free advice from the Internet, then I'd like to suggest that there are more effective ways of going about it!

In addition to identifying and learning new skills, you'll also have had those approaches, personality traits and so on which have carried you this far and which will carry you and your business forward into the future – these are valuable and to be leveraged.

As your business grew, you will also have found that there were attitudes, behaviours, and approaches that served you well in the past, but which are no longer useful: the ability to turn your hand to everything, for example, is something that you no longer need to have. If you've not found these, rest assured they are there– you've just not noticed them yet.

Be aware that not all of these things that you now must leave behind will have you breathing a sigh of relief. There will be things that you may have enjoyed doing, but which it's now time to delegate to someone else. It may have been great fun to write all your own marketing content, but now that you have someone on board to do that, you have to let it go. As they say here in Scotland – you don't buy a dog and bark yourself.

What else did you have to leave behind as you moved up the entrepreneurship ladder?

What do you need to let go of now?

This notion of 'learn, leverage or leave' is, in itself, pretty straightforward. In practice, however, like many things, it can be a little more difficult, not least because (I've said it before, I know) the only person you can't actually see is yourself, and we may not be fully aware of which skill or attribute is which. However keen our sense of self-awareness, we can never be quite sure how accurate our perception actually is, and it's essential that we gather feedback in order to be sure.

The obvious way to do this is to ask people that you know and trust will give you an honest answer what traits, approaches, behaviours, etc they see as helpful in propelling you forward. What do they feel holds you back? Listen for patterns in their answers. If several people are saying you have a tendency not to listen to others and to plough on with your own ideas, they can't all be wrong. This is probably something you must address. If they say that you communicate in an inspiring way that conveys purpose and meaning to what you're doing, then this is something to carry forward.

Where you can't ask people directly for whatever reason, or if you suspect that people are telling you what they think you want to hear rather than what they actually think of you, look closely at the responses you get from people. What results do your team deliver for you?

I learned several years ago that sometimes I really need to focus on explaining things more clearly than I think I need to. I'd delegate something to a team member with a bit of an explanation, and be surprised when they handed back a piece of work that was so far away from what I'd been expecting that it wasn't even funny.

To be honest, my initial thought was, "What's wrong with them, for goodness sake? I TOLD them what I wanted them to do!" Funnily enough, though, it kept happening – and not just with that team member, but with others, too. I started to wonder why they hadn't given me any feedback on my lack of clarity until it occurred to me that they didn't know how to delegate, either. The responsibility was mine to figure out.

The key thing here was that the results and responses I was getting represented a clear piece of feedback, and I'd suggest that you watch closely for feedback of this sort and once again look for patterns. What are people telling you that they aren't actually telling you? The signals are there if you look for them.

A while ago I coached a business owner who felt that although her team was good at following process and getting things done, they weren't proactive in solving problems, didn't really think out of the box, and tended to come to her for solutions. All of this was dragging her back into the day-to-day of her business, rather than allowing her the space needed to focus on strategy and growth.

These behaviours were 'feedback' on her leadership style, which was very process-focused. She'd developed systems for pretty much everything in the business and it was all extremely efficient. The flip side, though, was that people were used to following a process and doing what they were told. In effect, they had been 'trained' to not think out of the box or to be proactive. They just had to follow process. They didn't have to think for themselves, so why would they?

It was an enlightening moment for that business owner, and an indication that now was the time to leverage the strong processes that she had in place, whilst beginning to build a culture where creativity and a proactive approach to problem-solving became part of the way in which things were done.

Consider, then, a few vital questions about your own capability levels as you lead your growing business:

- What do you already know that you will carry forward on your entrepreneurial journey? What are the strengths you want to continue to employ?

- How will you leverage the skills of other people who will fill the gaps, bringing strengths to your business in areas where you are weak?

- What do you need or want to learn now as you take your business to the next level?

- What do you need to let go of that no longer serves you? What will you find most difficult to let go of?

CHAPTER SUMMARY:

- Look back on your journey so far and consider the skills you've had to learn, and the existing skills and traits which will carry you forward.

- Think very carefully indeed about what you must leave behind because it no longer serves you, or because it's time to delegate it to someone else.

- Ask for feedback from someone you trust rather than relying solely on your own perspective.

NOTES:

_____

_____

_____

_____

_____

_____

_____

_____

_____

_____

_____

_____

_____

_____

_____

_____

_____

_____

_____

_____

_____

_____

_____

CHAPTER 4

CHARACTER BUILDING STUFF

Your leadership character goes well beyond your personal brand. It's more about who you are with your team day by day than the impression you want to create of yourself outside your business.

You'll be very aware of some leaders – both current and historical –who inspired people to follow them through thick and thin, even when the odds seemed stacked against them.

These were leaders of great character.

Here we're going to take a look at your own leadership character – what it currently is and how you want to develop it – and your leadership legacy as you move forward.

Your personality

Your personality will have a strong impact and influence on your growing business: it can't help but be so. If you've taken personality profiler tests in the past (and there are more on the market than you can shake a stick at), dig out the results and refresh your memory on what they're telling you.

I'm using the term 'personality profiler' here as a general term. In practice, some profilers capture personality and others focus on behaviour. For example, Myers Briggs is a personality profiler ("I am an introvert") whereas DISC and others focus on behavioural style and how people are likely to respond in a given situation.

Many of the profilers are based on the work of Carl Jung, but one that's completely different is The Vitality Test by Nicholas Haines at the Five Institute. It's based on ancient Chinese energy systems and provides a very different and incredibly useful insight into who we are.

In reality, the more of these profilers that you do, the more you realise that they're all telling you pretty much the same thing. Patterns will start to emerge, and once you see them, you can't unsee them. Obviously, the accuracy of the results of any test of this sort is entirely dependent on the honesty and openness with which you answered the questions. It's important to capture what you actually do or think, not what you'd like to imagine you do or think. Whether or not you've taken any personality profilers in the past, they all tend to point in the same sort of direction.

'The Big Five', for example, covers (surprise, surprise) five factors which featured in many pieces of research over the years before being coined as a term by American psychologist Lewis Goldberg in the 1990s.

Consider where you sit on each of these lines, and seek a second opinion from someone you trust and who knows you well. It might give you a fresh perspective.

"THE BIG FIVE"

OPENNESS TO EXPERIENCE

Stick to what we know   Love the change!

CONSCIENTIOUSNESS

Disciplined and organised   Easygoing, spontaneous

EXTRAVERSION

Outgoing, energetic   Solitary, reserved

AGREEABLENESS

Friendly, approachable   Detached, challenging

NUEROTICISM

Sensitive, nervous   Secure, confident

As I've mentioned a few times now, the only person we can't actually see is ourselves, so while we might think we're pretty flexible in going with the flow during times of change, relative to others, we might be a bit of a stick-in-the-mud. We might feel secure and confident most of the time, but sometimes we're triggered to be more sensitive.

Remember, we're doing this exercise to build our self-awareness, not to put ourselves into a box. If we don't have an accurate view of ourselves, we'll be making life – and business – more difficult for ourselves in the long run. We'll start getting results that we don't understand because we just don't see how we're having an impact on our environment, and on those around us.

Looking at The Big Five, then, where would you put yourself on each of the lines?

Think back to particular situations when you've acted in a particular way (ACTUAL situations, in other words, rather than giving it your best guess). An instinctive response to questions about self often delivers an answer that indicates what we would like to think we do rather than what we actually do... and there can be a significant difference between the two.

If you're generally at a particular point on the line, what triggers you to move in either direction? Perhaps a response to someone or something? Recognising these triggers follows the same principle as when we considered courage and confidence: if we're aware of what causes us to move, we can manage ourselves better.

More than that, we can start to recognise where other people's approaches differ from ours, and change our own response to and communication style with them in order to build better relationships.

Consider also this slightly different mix of parameters, which appear in various guises in a number of other profilers. Which of these factors do you tend to focus on and consider most important... or is it a mix?

- The task, and the results to be achieved ("Let's get on with it! We've got work to do!")

- The people involved ("Is everyone on board and OK?")

- The detail and the data ("What's the process? What are the facts?")

- The vision and the 'big picture' goal ("It's going to be great! We're heading to the promised land!")

Many people will find that their preferences are a mix of more than one, but often a person will find that they have a strong preference for one over the others. You'll also notice that a strong team needs all of these approaches in the mix, not just one or two.

Awareness of this is critical. If you're someone for whom task and results are a priority, be aware that someone with a very different personality (a people person, say) might view you as a heartless slave-driver as you press towards success and seem less concerned about whether or not you're taking everyone with you. A detail and data person might see you as an impetuous risk-taker, because you're not, in their view, taking enough time to gather all the possible facts. A vision and purpose person might see you as someone with no higher values because it seems to them that you're about results at all costs.

These perceptions aren't necessarily true, of course, but the thing is, when we're under pressure, we tend to revert to our default selves – and more than that, we tend to become irrationally judgemental of those who view the world differently.

Watch out for this. Being aware of your own style is merely the first step. Anyone who's ever completed a personality profiler and become absorbed in the "Look at me! I'm SUCH an xyz!" side of it is missing a key point: it's not just about who you are; it's about who everyone else is, and how you relate to them.

Building this type of understanding of yourself and others is a wise move which will stand you in good stead as you build your business, and establish your true character as a leader.

A good way to gain better understanding of other people (and their preferences and personality), is to listen closely – not just to what they say, but to how they say it. What do they focus on? If, for example, they're talking about their weekend, are they talking about what they achieved – a personal best in the local park run, for example? Are they focused on the social side, and the people they met up with?

I have a friend who will say something like, "It's 5 degrees colder today than it was at this time yesterday!" because he's a numbers and detail person. As more of a big picture thinker, my observation is, "It's Baltic! I'll need an extra sweater!" and I don't really think about the specifics.

Listen very closely, because people are giving you clues as to their own personality and preferences all the time.

Reflect back on your life and your business journey so far, and consider:

- Where has your personality and your approach had the biggest impact in your life, for good or for bad?

- Where has it had the biggest impact in your business?

- What do you notice, on reflection, about the personalities of others you know or work with?

Your leadership character

Your leadership character– your leadership brand, if you will – is a combination of a few factors: how you see yourself, how you act and put yourself across, and how others perceive you. And it's important not to be too quick to assume that other people see you in the same way that you see yourself.

Again, reflect on the response that you tend to get from the people around you, either directly or indirectly.

- What words do your team associate with you? What words do you WANT them to associate with you?

- How do your team describe your style?

- What impact do you tend to have on people? When you leave them, are they inspired? More knowledgeable? Happier? Or full of self-doubt, fear for the future or worry?!

Think carefully about the leader you want to become, and what you have to do – or perhaps what you have to change – to become this person.

I'd suggest you take a piece of paper and divide it into two. On one side, write the heading, "The leadership impact I want to have", and think about it. How DO you want to be seen by others? Inspiring? Results-driven? Purposeful?

Once you have a list under this heading, think carefully about what you need to do and who you need to be to be seen as this leadership character. Be honest about what you may need to change, and what you may need to learn, leverage or leave in order to do this.

Leadership Impact I Want To Have	Behaviours, Attitude, Approaches
Inspiring	Communicating with more impact, and not just focusing on the task at hand
Strong leader	Set clear goals. Give feedback, both positive and negative to keep the team on track.
Purposeful	Clarify what our purpose is, and make sure everyone understands this

CHAPTER SUMMARY:

- Consider your own personality and preferences: are you focused on tasks and results, data and detail, the big picture and values, or people?

- Listen closely, not just to what people say, but how they express themselves. This will give you clues as to their personality type and preferences.

- Consider how you want to be perceived, and what you may have to do in order to be seen in this way.

NOTES:

_____

_____

_____

_____

_____

_____

_____

_____

_____

_____

_____

_____

_____

_____

_____

_____

_____

_____

_____

_____

_____

_____

PEA # 2

PURPOSE

*"Leaders establish the vision for the future
and set the strategy for getting there."*

John P Kotter

CHAPTER 5

WHAT'S HIDING...

We're going to turn our attention to your business now, looking at the higher-level factors like purpose, business values, vision and mission, and on articulating these clearly and in a way that your team (and clients, but let's focus internally for now) understand, buy into and most importantly, live and work by.

We'll kick-start the thinking process by asking some pretty fundamental questions:

- What exactly are you doing?

- Why and how are you doing it?

- Who cares?

- Does everyone in your business know all of this?!

It should be obvious why we've focused on you as a person first: if you're the business founder, your business purpose and values will mirror your personal purpose and values. Your skills and preferences will inevitably have shaped your business from the very beginning, for better and for worse.

If you've taken over or bought a company, the business values and purpose will in some way mirror your own, otherwise you wouldn't have been drawn to it – either that, or you will consciously or subconsciously be influencing your business to conform to your values and worldview. It's something that just happens.

Even if the critical high-level factors that we're about to look at are already in place, it's worth reviewing them to make sure they are an accurate reflection of who you are and where you're going as a business, and that this is all clearly understood by everyone in your team.

This latter part – ensuring that everyone else knows what's going on – is often overlooked as businesses grow, and leaders take the easy option of providing instructions rather than sharing goals, direction and purpose.

Don't make that mistake. It won't serve you in the long run.

The factors we're considering in this chapter – purpose, vision, mission, and values – aren't just 'nice to haves' or 'touchy-feely stuff'. They will have a profound impact on your business as it grows in both seen and unseen ways. How you manage your team, your brand and culture, working practices, decision-making... many day-to-day business activities are at stake, so don't take them lightly.

Perhaps the more important thing here is that nature abhors a vacuum, and will fill it with something. As the business leader, if you're not actively clarifying and implementing these things, something else will fill the gap and provide its own answers, and you might not like what they are.

I'll just say it again for those at the back who didn't hear: it's absolutely imperative that your team know and deeply understand the key points of your purpose, direction and strategy, and their part in these.

Please don't take for granted that they have the same concept of why your business exists as you do: SO many businesses have staff who, when asked questions about why the business exists, will say something like, "So Rick can buy a new car every year" or some such. Yes, these things are probably said as a bit of a joke, but as the old saying goes, "Many a true word is spoken in jest." Your team's FIRST response to this question should be a genuine one, not a flippant one.

They MUST know who you are as a business, as well as what you do.

Don't be tempted to brush off this crucial factor by telling yourself "of course they do" and moving on.

Ask them. You might be surprised.

...BELOW THE WATER LINE?

It's very easy to get caught up in the day-to-day hustle and bustle of life and business and lose sight of who we are and what we're here for. You don't have to look too far to find corporate examples of this. From time to time an ambitious new CEO forges forward with bold new directions to take the company in...but these aren't in line with who the company actually is and are at odds with its brand values, and the initiative eventually flounders.

Who are you, as a business?

Clarifying base-level factors such as who you are, why you exist, whom you serve and what you do will provide a foundation and a touchstone which everyone can understand and buy into. They will underpin your core values, purpose, vision and mission.

So let's dive on in and explore some of these broader factors before distilling them down to core statements of what your business is and what it stands for.

Why does your business exist?

For some people, their business exists because they inherited it, or because it was an obvious extension of whatever they studied in college.

If it's the former, it's worth considering what's prompted you to take on the business. As a word to the wise, for your own job satisfaction it'd be best if you didn't just see it as a gravy train and an easy income, or feel an obligation to your parents, as can happen with family businesses. What else? How does it actually fulfil you?

If you're the founder, what prompted you to start THIS business, rather than something else? It may be that you spotted a gap in the market, or that it's what you studied after school or university, or that you leveraged a hobby or an interest to build a business, or something else.

Whatever the circumstances, give some thought to your reason 'why THIS business'. It may seem like an abstract question, but answering the fundamental question of "why are we/am I doing this?" can be a useful touchstone when the going gets tough. If you have a strong reason 'why', it can be your compass in the storm.

A short while ago, I was struck when a programme participant told me that the founder of his company, back in the day, had articulated a very strong 'why'.

The company was in the healthcare sector, and the 'why' was: "There is work to be done...and the patients are waiting."

That last phrase was one that all staff could identify with: patients are waiting. Time is of the essence. Lives are at stake.

A strong why, indeed.

And what of your team? Do they really know why your business exists and what the ultimate purpose is...beyond making money?

Current research indicates clearly that staff (as well as clients) who connect with a business's purpose are more productive, more dedicated and more likely to stay with your company. There is, in other words, a firm connection to your bottom line.

Whom do you serve?

I'm assuming that, having reached a level within your business, you're not someone who claims "It's for everyone." If you are, I'd suggest that you speak to a strategist or branding expert pretty quickly.

The point of this question isn't about branding per se, or about whom you COULD serve (which may indeed be pretty much anyone). It's about whom you serve best and indeed want to serve, and who your products best benefit – your IDEAL potential clients, in other words.

Variously referred to as a marketing persona or an ideal client avatar, depending on who you speak to, the basic criteria are that:

- they have a need for what you provide
- what you provide actually benefits them
- they have the money to pay you for it
- they're the sort of people/businesses you'd want to work with.

To some degree, these are statements of the obvious, but as you grow and scale your business, it's important to take a fresh look at who you're actually working with versus who you'd rather work with; which customers/clients are likely to generate more revenue, as opposed to which ones tend to be chancers who take up unnecessary time and make life difficult; and so on.

Why? Because sales aren't going to increase exponentially by working harder and faster and doing more 'stuff'; they're going to increase significantly by being strategic. To use a cliché: by working smarter, not harder.

At this point, I suggest you undertake a bit of an audit to give yourself a clear view of your current client base. Who are your actual current clients? Who are your IDEAL clients, moving forward?

As you consider this, think back to the work you did in the Personal section. What does your business need to do for you? What are your values? What are your personal purpose and aspirations? How do these impact who your ideal clients might be?

The table below will help you to frame your thoughts. Some of the factors relate more to the individual making the purchasing decision than to the business itself. Just adapt your answers as you see fit.

This level of detail might look like overkill at first glance, but go with it. People buy from people, and it's important that you and everyone on your team sees your clients and purchasers as human beings, and not just job titles. Thinking about all this now will help inform and target your marketing efforts later on.

Where you have different client types, complete a separate form for each type.

For example, Scott, a client of mine, owns a property management company, and as such has different client types: landlords who wish to rent out their properties, businesses who want to take on a property over several months for visiting project staff or contractors, and holidaymakers who want to book a property for a short-term stay.

Each of these client types has different needs and wants, and within these three categories, there are some clients who generate more revenue than others, who are repeat buyers, and so on.

Once you've looked at whom you're currently serving and who you'd LIKE to serve in your future business, it'll be easier to see where you may need to shift the focus of your strategy.

Factor	Current client	IDEAL client
Age		
Demographic		
Business sector		
Business characteristics		
Location		
Average spend		
Brands they align with		
Business concerns		
Life concerns		
Business		
Problems		
Life problems		
Business aspirations		
Life aspirations		

Considering your ideal client in this detail might seem like overkill, but it isn't: to stress the point again, it'll be vital to your marketing efforts and to your overall customer focus to see them as people and not just a demographic or type.

Once again (and this question is going to come up a few times in the coming pages), what of your team? Do they really know their clients and whom they serve? Do they see them as actual people... or as a mass of statistics or an amorphous group of 'engineers' or 'HR executives' or whatever it might be?

A few years ago, I was in the early stages of working with a client, and was speaking to staff to clarify their ideas about their customer base. When I asked the question, "Whom do you serve?" at least three people in the group said, "Jo Bloggs", and gave the name of the CEO. It was mildly amusing, but whilst it might have been gratifying to the CEO, it certainly wasn't useful to the business.

Don't let this be you. Your team MUST keep your customers in mind, even if they aren't in a customer-facing role.

Global corporates that I've worked with over the years have invested significantly in programmes to ensure that ALL staff remain customer-centric, and keep in mind whom they actually serve. Senior executives in such firms often accomplish this by spending a day or so shadowing teams who are customer-facing, or sitting in on calls at the call centre, or going on site visits – whatever brings them closer to the front lines and the clients they serve.

One participant in a leadership programme I was delivering for Avon Cosmetics years ago hailed from the finance team. He was a bit of a character and a joy to work with, contributing a great deal to the learning experience of his fellow delegates.

One of the things he said has stayed with me all these years. I'd asked him what he'd wanted to get out of the programme. His reply?

"I wanted to remind myself that I work for a company that provides an income opportunity for women by selling cosmetics... not sheets of paper with numbers on them."

Your team having a clear idea of whom they serve will keep them connected to everything they do, giving them a personal sense of purpose and contributing to a customer-centred focus within your business.

Yes, yes... you'll need to be focused on building business equity and shareholder focus, too – but remember at all times who's actually paying the bills.

How do you serve?

Many companies seem to have a rather vague and generic approach to expressing how they serve their customers, claiming to be "Providing the best in xyz", or, my pet peeve phrase: "Best in class", which sounds more like a breed champion at a dog show than anything relevant to business.

Others often express something about operating with "reliability and honesty", and this doesn't go all the way either, in my view. Frankly, if you're not operating reliably and honestly, you shouldn't be in business. Having to specify that makes you look even more shifty.

The point is to re-think and re-articulate how you serve your clients and customers in a way that cements it in the minds of clients and staff, so that everyone is on the same page.

Spell it out. Don't leave anyone guessing, and make sure your team is clear on what it is about your approach that makes you different, so it becomes part of their own belief system.

- What exactly do you do for your customers and clients, and how do you create value?
- What methods and approaches have you developed?
- What results do you get for people?
- What's unique about the way in which you do things?

And two further questions that may make you inwardly squirm:

- Why should anyone care?
- Why would they want to come to you rather than go to someone else?

Deep thought is needed to clarify these points, and gathering feedback from existing clients will add valuable data to the mix. Invest a little time in thinking it through, or on clarifying the answers that you already have.

HOW you do what you do may well be your Unique Selling Point, setting you apart from the 'also-rans' who are in the same line of business as you are, but don't do things like you do.

What do you actually do to serve?

This is often where people go first when they are articulating what they do. Obviously, at a basic, transactional level, it's the bare bones of the service you provide.

In my view, it's best not to jargon this up too much. I once met someone at a conference who said she was a 'development solutions architect', and I was completely baffled. Turns out she wrote training courses.

Aside from the basic thing that you do, it's valuable if everyone in your business can see how their role impacts this. They might not be the person with the spanner in their hand fixing the aircraft fuel gauge, for example. They might be the person on the cleaning team ensuring that the surrounding area remains clean and uncontaminated, thereby making their own contribution to the working environment, and ultimately to safety in the skies. Or the legal assistant ensuring that compliance standards are met so that the business continues to operate efficiently and appropriately... thereby contributing to safety in the skies. Or the forklift truck driver, ensuring that parts are moved carefully from one part of the plant to the other, thereby contributing to safety in... you get the picture.

Being clear about what the business does, for whom and why, and ensuring that everyone understands this can help minimise silos later on by focusing minds on higher-level goals and purpose.

Conflict will always arise at some point, but it will be less angst-ridden if everyone can quickly concur on their common goals as a starting point.

Your business values, vision and mission

Much of what we've looked at in this section can be distilled into core statements of who you are, why you exist and what you stand for.

Don't mistake these statements for unnecessary corporate guff: a clear and honest statement can be powerful in uniting your team in pursuit of a common goal and forging a deeper connection with their personal values and aspirations.

Your business values

As the business founder, your business values will probably be in line with your own personal values.

Your values will be part of your brand and culture, and if correctly articulated, will form part of your performance management processes, your decision-making and many other day-to-day activities.

One of the worst things that can happen is for a list of nice words to become a poster on the wall but have no link to real working life within that business. Trust, honesty, integrity, service... those things mean nothing if they aren't actively implemented in some way in your business.

The worst example I've ever seen of this (and I'm not going to name the client!) was in the finance sector. I only worked with them once, and never went back. All of the marketing material spoke warmly of valuing people, acting with integrity, caring for factors beyond the money they were handling – the usual stuff. Behind closed doors, however, it was the most toxic culture I've ever witnessed. Staff lived in a state of fear, a blame culture was endemic, and stress levels were high. It wasn't unusual for a manager to step out of their office and shout at staff members in front of the whole team, whilst those around them cowered at their desks, thanking their lucky stars that it wasn't them in the firing line this time. Staff turnover was high.

Suppliers were lied to and treated with disdain – heck, a legal department made a point of going through contracts with a fine-toothed comb to look for loopholes so that they could avoid paying for services.

They might have been claiming trust and integrity as their values, but in reality they were operating by 'anti-values' of abuse of power, fear and blame. And it was horrible to see.

In complete contrast, I've worked with other companies, large and small, whose values are genuine, and are woven into the fabric of their culture and how they do business. The upshot? Lower staff turnover, higher levels of motivation, higher productivity and a quantifiable benefit to the bottom line.

Your business values matter profoundly – so what are they?

At their root, they should be factors which you'd want your team to adhere to no matter what. This is why many larger organisations adopt broad-reaching concepts like 'authenticity', 'trust' and so on, and back these up by being specific about what this actually means in real life, rather than relying on vague notions of abstract concepts. These will almost certainly align with the personal values that we looked at in Pea # 1.

Broad-reaching concepts like 'trust' work well when they are:

- Clearly defined and translated into a set of behavioural 'guiding principles' which people are measured on (more about that in Pea # 5: Paradigms later).

- Spoken about often and brought into the culture of the organisation.

- 'Layered' and worked in combination with core strategic messages and purpose, vision and mission.

- Role modelled by leaders. (This one is possibly the most vital.)

In other words, they are real, they are in evidence day to day, and they actually mean something.

Where this doesn't work (or is at best pointless), is where there are a few fancy words on a poster or some corporate material, but where actual behaviours and practices are completely different in real life.

So, looking to the future:

- What core values do you want your business to hold?

- How would people in your business be behaving towards customers and working together if they upheld this value?

- What sacrifices are you prepared to make as a business to uphold these values?

- If you aren't... are they really your values?

Looking at the present, it's not too difficult to see what values are currently at play in your business by looking closely at what people are actually DOing. Not just talking about – but doing.

- What are the values that your business is currently demonstrating?

For example, if you'd like your team to work in a spirit of trust, but at the moment everyone seems intent on stabbing their colleagues in the back to get ahead, then the actual 'value' isn't trust at all. It's something like 'win at all costs'. Or, more positively, if everyone will step in to help a colleague who's struggling to meet a delivery deadline for a client, they're clearly acting with teamwork and collaboration in mind.

- How well do you and your leadership team role model these values? Consistently?

- What reasons (excuses) do you make when you don't?

- What values are you ACTUALLY living and breathing in your business, as evidenced by observable behaviours and results?

What values will your business commit to, not sacrifice for profit, and be prepared to champion in the face of challenge?

Write them down. Make a commitment that this is what you stand for.

Writing your vision and mission and values statements

Many people scoff at these statements, writing them off as corporate nonsense. To be fair, as with the business values, where they are a marketing puff piece that bears no relation to reality, they're probably right.

Where they are a clear iteration of a company's purpose, its current trajectory and the values it genuinely stands for, though, they can be a powerful force in uniting staff and clients under a single banner.

Let's not get dragged into more of the semantics here, though – I hear a lot of unnecessary questions in workshops about what these statements should contain, which of them are future-focused and which are focused on the present.

To me, the key point is this: you must distil your thinking into a set of core statements that genuinely represent what you stand for.

- Your Vision: the world you're seeking to create. (e.g. "A world without cancer.")

- Your Mission: your own objective in relation to this, and what you're doing to move towards it. (e.g. "Tirelessly seeking the cure through funded research programmes.")

People don't believe blandishments and corporate jargon, so give them something real: a banner to rally to, something that you and your business stand for, and something that they can stand for, as well.

By way of example, my own vision is for happy and fulfilled business owners to be running successful, profitable businesses that contribute to the wider community and to the economy.

My mission is to provide real-life, practical support to business leaders through consultancy, coaching and training, using The 5 Peas Framework™ – growing businesses, building leaders... and changing lives.

- What are your vision and mission?
- How well does your team understand this?
- How well does your business currently reflect this?
- What needs to change?

CHAPTER SUMMARY:

- Your vision, mission, purpose, values, and other high-level factors provide a backdrop for your business strategy.
- Effort at this stage to clarify these factors will reap dividends later on, as you build your culture and manage your team's performance.
- It's easy to get caught up in the vocabulary of strategy: is it a vision or a mission? An objective or a goal? It doesn't matter what you call it – you must have a clear statement of purpose and intent.
- There is no room for corporate jargon in these high-level statements. They must mean something and use vocabulary that people would be happy to use if explaining the business to their friends in a social setting.

NOTES:

CHAPTER 6

VISION INTO ACTION

What we've covered so far in Pea #2 can be seen as the 'beating heart' of your business: without a clear iteration of these, your business becomes a soulless machine.

We also need the 'head' part to function efficiently, and as a visual device for collating, analysing and evaluating where you currently are and where you're going, Alexander Osterwalder's Business Model Canvas is excellent.

Writing anything down in this way – especially if you're able to involve your leadership team – will focus you on being defined and succinct, and clear up any misunderstandings and inaccuracies that might have cropped up in people's minds.

There's something specific that I'm going to suggest you do here. Let's go through it first, though.

THE BUSINESS MODEL CANVAS: CURRENT ACTUAL

KEY PARTNERS	KEY ACTIVITIES	VALUE PROPOSITION	CUSTOMER RELATIONSHIP	CUSTOMER SEGMENTS
	KEY RESOURCES		CHANNELS	
COST STRUCTURE		REVENUE STREAMS		

To explain the terms:

Value Proposition (in the middle): What value do you provide to customers and clients? What results do you offer? What problems do you solve? What aspirations do you help them to achieve?

Partners: Who works with you in the delivery of what you do? Suppliers? Partners? Associates?

Activities: What activities are needed to deliver your value proposition? Distribution? Customer service?

Key Resources: What resources does your value proposition require?

Customer Segment: Who's your customer...your IDEAL customer vs. your actual customer?

Customer Relationships: What relationships do your clients expect? What do you do to provide this?

Distribution Channels: How do you reach and serve your clients and customers?

Cost Structure: What are your main business costs and how do they relate to your revenue streams?

Revenue Streams: What do your customers pay for? What are your different revenue streams? What's the value of each stream?

What I suggest is for you to do this three-stage activity. It's something I often do in workshops with my clients to make sure that they are clear and aligned, and that everyone is on the same page. Clarity and alignment – these are the watchwords here.

Don't take for granted that your leadership team will all have the same understanding of where you're going. Talk it out and make sure.

I was taking a strategy workshop where the leadership team had been asked in advance to describe their aspirations for the business, independent of each other. As we talked it through, they were pretty pleased with themselves: all had spoken about building the company to an 'optimum size' and about 'increasing revenue' and becoming 'a respected voice in their sector'.

What became clear when we started to dig under the surface of all this, though, was that everyone had a different understanding of what these things actually meant. One saw 'optimum size' as around 60 people, while another was aiming for 80. One was ambitious for 30% growth as an aspiration. One was happy to settle for an incremental 12%.

Whilst they seemed to be in agreement, in fact, they were all working towards very different things...something which would have created problems and misunderstandings if we hadn't ironed them out at this stage and ensured that there was crystal clear understanding and agreement on what everyone – the entire business – was aiming for.

Involve your leadership team, then, in this activity:

1) First, complete an imaginary Business Model Canvas for how you would like your business to be in 3 or 5 or 10 years' time – pick a timeframe that makes sense to you. Filling in as many of the details as possible will force you to think about what you actually want for your business, rather than the vague 'double-digit growth' or 'x% over y years' that people often fall back on.

Challenge yourself to nail your colours to the mast and to capture your aspirations. Look back at your goals in the 'Personal' section and make sure that they align, and that your future business isn't at odds with your personal aspirations.

My preference is always to draw these things out on a large whiteboard or a flipchart or something, not to just work on a piece of A4, and to type it up afterwards, once you've done with rubbing out and re-scribbling a few things. Better still – leave it up on the wall for a few days: it's amazing how thoughts occur to you as you walk past it in the 72 hours after you first wrote it up.

The background thinking that you've already done on purpose, vision, mission and values will pave the way for this. It's essential that it's approached with honesty and with real consideration. If it's treated as a box-ticking, fill-in-the-gaps exercise, it'll be a waste of time.

2) Next, complete a Business Model Canvas for your business as it stands today – an accurate, no-holds-barred view of your business as it is, not what you'd like to think it is.

Dig out your data and details and put them all in one place so that you can comprehensively see what's going on.

Again, involve your leadership team (if you have one), to ensure that you get different perspectives on the status quo, rather than just relying on your own viewpoint.

3) Place the two Business Model Canvasses side by side:

- What's the difference?

- What do you already have in place that you want to keep? What has to change?

- What has to change first, or soonest?

Identifying which things need to happen first will become your strategic priorities for the next 12-18 months.

The next stage is to align all areas of your business towards achieving them, and to craft your strategy.

Setting your strategy

In defining your growth strategy, it's not all about the internal factors and what you want to happen: external factors are also critical.

When was the last time you stuck your head above the parapet to see what was on the horizon?

I have some clients who are extremely good at this, and are constantly scanning for opportunities or hazards that might take them towards or impede them from achieving their overall objectives. But there are also companies that we've all seen focus inwards, miss the signs, and pay the price for doing so: Kodak, Blockbuster Video...you don't have to look far.

Focus on some of the external factors that directly or indirectly affect your business:

1. Look at the work you did in the Business Model Canvas exercise and hold that thought.

2. Carry out a 'PESTILED' analysis to assess the impact of the following on your business:

- Political factors: Changes of government or policy

- Economic factors: Is your sector in a boom or bust state, or something in between?

- Social factors: What cultural or social factors are at work?

- Technological factors: What recent research and development, software, etc may have an impact on you?

- International factors: What's the global perspective? What's happening elsewhere in the world?

- Legal factors: Are there changes in legislation that might impact your plans?

- Environmental factors: What's the environmental impact?

- Demographic factors: What are current trends in the demographic that you serve?

3. Competitor Analysis: Consider not just your immediate competitors, but those with whom you compete for time and money.

4. In light of the above, what are your company's Strengths, Weaknesses, Opportunities and Threats? Involve your team in this SWOT analysis. (Yes, it's an approach we're familiar with, but there's a reason for it: it's a good temperature check of where you are.)

How much actual data do you have on all this?

What do you need to find out?

THE PLAN COMES TOGETHER

Once you – and each member of your leadership team – is clear on who you are and where you're all going and the external factors that will impact your business, we come to the point of turning aspirations into some sort of a plan of action. A strategy.

Again, language sometimes works against us. I've facilitated many workshops where participants will ask, "Is this a strategy or a goal? Or perhaps an objective?"

Don't get caught up in the semantics. The focus here is on taking higher-level aspirations and funnelling them down into what needs to be done to actually get there. You can call it whatever you like, frankly.

What we're working towards here will cover all aspects of your business, and it's where knowing yourself and understanding your own Capabilities and Character will come in.

Why? Because your instinct – everybody's instinct – is to focus on the things that you enjoy and are good at, and prioritise them. If you're a process person, you'll be driven to focus on getting your processes in place, and maybe miss some of the people aspects. If you're sales or results-driven, you may be intent on driving sales, sales, sales...and less on building the infrastructure that will support the delivery of your service.

Your plans must place equal emphasis on each area of your business. If your strategic priorities are to achieve X by Y according to your future Business Model Canvas, think about what needs to happen in terms of:

- Sales and Marketing
- Finance
- HR and Admin
- Customer Service, Operations and Service Delivery

You may have more departments or functions, of course – this just covers the basics. Each function must have a clear strategy, purpose and direction of its own that feeds into the overall. And they must work and communicate cross-functionally so that silos don't develop.

Within each function, your leadership team will take the lead on:

- The sub-strategy for that department or function that feeds into the overall strategy, in pursuance of the overall mission and vision.
- Who's involved, their goals, roles and responsibilities, and how they are being managed.
- The processes, systems and tools that must be in place to support them.

From here, you can go on to consider individual goals, ensuring that everyone maintains a line of sight towards what they do day to day, and the overall vision, mission and strategy. We'll look at this in the 'Pea # 3: People' section.

Just to be clear, here's where we are in the grand scheme of things:

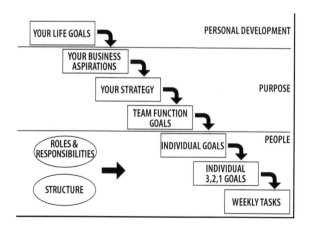

Be clear on the long game

Check that you're clear on the long-term game that you're playing here. Whilst you might not want to look decades ahead from the present, your strategy will be different depending on whether you're looking to grow a business to pass on to your kids, versus employee ownership, versus looking for investment at the five-year mark, versus selling up at ten years in. Even at this stage, having an idea of your exit strategy, and where you're ultimately working towards, is useful.

We can't ignore the fact that things change, both internally and externally, but having a clear purpose, clarity and direction is crucial.

You may think this is stating the obvious, but perhaps it is less so when considering the fact that this must be a clear and well-communicated goal (especially among your leadership team, as they must then communicate these aspects further down your business).

Bear in mind also that in the background there's a balance to be struck between building equity in your business, maintaining employee engagement, managing supplier relations, and remaining customer-focused. If one of these become prominent at the expense of the others, problems will arise.

12-18 months

Considering your longer-term goals and vision, what needs to happen in the next 12-18 months in order to move forward towards these?

These are your strategic priorities, and you and your leadership team need to clarify what each department or function needs to do to meet your agenda.

I'm a great believer in keeping it simple, and in distilling the strategic plan down to its essence, fitting the key points on a single page:

12-18 Months

Strategic aims for next 12-18 months

Teams/Functions

Marketing	Sales	Finance	Operations	Etc etc

Key Deliverables

1.	1.	1.	1.	1.
2.	2.	2.	2.	2.
3.	3.	3.	3.	3.

Team/Function goals

Whatever you decide are the priorities for each function as you drive towards your strategy, look at the cross-functional impact: if you're looking for increased sales or a new market as part of your strategy, how will that affect the service/product delivery team? IT? Finance? Make sure that EVERYONE is ready for the growth that you anticipate.

Focus on the set of goals that each function will have, feeding into the overall 12-18 month plan, agree what the key priorities and measurables will be, and iron out any apparent conflict between functions/teams (or agree how these will be tackled when they arise).

Bear in mind that there are some things which are, and always will be, EVERYONE's responsibility:

- Everyone in your business must understand how they contribute to the bottom line, so that they are aware of the financial impact of decisions they make and can be good stewards of their resources – that's not just finance's job.

- Everyone is a champion of your brand and your values – not just marketing.

- Everyone is responsible for good people practices and sound management – not just HR.

Begin to instil these factors into your culture as early as possible, and you'll be ahead of most corporates that I've worked with over the years.

Breaking this down further, each function leader will define their own plan, in relation to the strategy:

TEAM/FUNCTION

Key deliverables

1.	2.	3.

Key Activities

Key Measures

VALUES AND BEHAVIOURS

Note that I've included values and behaviours in the mix. As with most things in life, it's not just about what you do; it's about the way in which you do it.

Communication

Consider, as early as you can, what your communication infrastructure will be. As your business grows, communication will become the biggest challenge (trust me, it will). Set precedents and good practices in motion now and it'll stand you in good stead in the future.

With this communication in mind, consider:

- How will different functions communicate on key actions and activities to ensure that they are pulling in the same direction? Meetings? Briefings? Bulletins? Make sure you have a good mix of communication methods to ensure that key messages get to the people who need them, are understood, and are acted upon (not just emailed and left to chance).

- Where might there be conflict between functions or teams? (For example, finance might be tasked with saving money whilst marketing might want an increase in spending to meet its goals.)

- How will these potential areas of conflict be addressed?

- How will you promote a 'whole business first' mentality, so that individuals or functions don't start to put their priorities above the business as a whole? (Yes, it happens!)

All of this will cascade down into specific goals and activities for team members in 3 month, 2 month, 1 month plans ('321 plans') – something we'll cover in 'Pea # 3: People'.

CHAPTER SUMMARY:

- Keep your high-level aspirations and the results of your Business Model Canvas activity in mind as you focus on actionable goals.

- Consider external as well as internal factors that will impact you and your team's ability to deliver your strategy.

- Consider what each function/area of your business needs to do to deliver on your strategy, and where there might be crossover or conflict.

- Think carefully about how you communicate your strategy, and ensure everyone's understanding of their part in it.

NOTES:

_____

_____

_____

_____

_____

_____

_____

_____

_____

_____

_____

_____

_____

_____

_____

_____

_____

_____

_____

_____

_____

_____

PEA # 3

PEOPLE

"If you want to do really important and big things in life, you can't do anything by yourself."

Deepak Chopra

CHAPTER 7

WHO'S ON THE BUS?

Your people are at the heart of your business. Even if you don't feel that you're a 'people person' or you don't do the 'touchy-feely stuff', it's absolutely imperative that you understand the people you have in your team, and how human beings function generally. This doesn't require a psychology degree – all that's needed is simple curiosity, a bit of patience and some observation skills.

WHO ARE THEY AND WHERE?

Before diving into the strategy cascade, individual goal-setting and people management side, though, let's take a step back and look at the current structure of your business: who's on board and where are they now, and what the structure needs to look like to deliver on the strategy and the future-focused business model canvas, as we reviewed in the last section. Inevitably, your business structure will change as you grow.

This isn't necessarily a linear thought process; this is about gathering data, spreading it out on the table in front of you, and piecing it together like a jigsaw. The result will form a picture of your current organisational structure, and the goal is to understand what that structure will need to be in order to support your future growth strategy.

Keep in mind that you and your leadership team are also team members, and very much part of the mix. I used to ask managers in my workshops, "How many people are in your team?" They'd come up with a number and I'd follow up with, "Did you include yourself in that number?" Most of them hadn't. It's a frequent oversight, and one to avoid.

Let's start where you are now, though, with the people you currently have with you.

- Who's on board?
- Where are they?
- Where do they need to be?
- What do they need to do?

Who's on board?

The team you have around you now – the bold adventurers who have staked their careers on working with you in your growing business rather than taking safer options elsewhere – are the bedrock and the springboard for your growth.

It's worth taking a close look at who's on board, and what their contribution to the business is, not just to get a snapshot of the 'human resources' you currently have, but to scrutinise the skills at your disposal. In most businesses (scale-ups in particular), staff often find themselves with official and unofficial roles, and now is a good time to get a handle on it all.

I suggest undertaking a 'People Inventory', capturing information on who you have now, and what they currently do. Before you do this, you MUST explain to your team what you're doing and why: to take stock of who you have on board and who you may need to train or bring into the team as you grow.

People Inventory

NAME:	JOB TITLE:	REPORTS TO:
'OFFICIAL' TASKS:		'UNOFFICAL' TASKS:
MEASURED ON:		
NOT MEASURED ON:		

People Inventory

NAME:	JOB TITLE:	REPORTS TO:
CAPABILITY (ON A SCALE OF 1-10) EVIDENCED BY:		AREAS FOR GROWTH:
BELIEF SYSTEM MATCHES COMPANY VALUES (ON A SCALE OF 1-10)		
EVIDENCED BY:		AREAS FOR GROWTH:
ATTITUDE (ON A SCALE OF 1-10) EVIDENCED BY:		AREAS FOR GROWTH:

What these 'People Inventories' will do is this:

- Highlight any differences in what you think people do and what they actually do, so that you can clarify and confirm that everyone actually IS working on something that moves you towards your goals, and is in alignment with your values.

- Show you what people think they're measured on...and highlight what they could/should be measured on. This will be important going forward when you're keeping people on track with business goals.

- Indicate what people think their development needs are (following a straightforward 'CBA' framework: Capability, Belief Systems and Aptitude).This will help you to plan how you might meet those needs, to ensure everyone is fully equipped to deliver your strategy.

(By Capability, I mean the skills, knowledge and understanding that people need to be able to do their job. By Belief Systems, I mean their values, how these connect with your business values, and what in their approach and behaviour demonstrates to you that this is the case. By Aptitude, I mean their potential to grow with your business, and perhaps step into a future leadership role.)

- Help you to establish which elements of your people plan will need documentation and which are more fluid.

When we move on to look at what and who you'll need to deliver your future vision, this exercise will be a stake in the ground, and give you a clearer idea of whether to hire, outsource, or train someone you already have.

Encouraging team members to assess themselves will set the tone for future performance management and goal-tracking, and encourage a culture of openness and self-reflection.

Here's what to do:

- Complete a People Inventory worksheet for each of your team, following the example above – either doing this yourself or getting your leadership team to fill one in for each of their direct reports. Be thorough: now is not the time for shortcuts.

- At the same time, ask each of your team members to complete one for themselves and return it to you. Remember to explain why you're asking them to do this. If people feel threatened, they won't respond honestly!

- When you have everyone's responses, and you've completed your own inventories on your team, sit down with your leadership team and compare the results between what you think people are doing/capable of, and what your team members have written about themselves.

- Set aside time to speak to each of your team members to go over their inventories. You may have questions to ask them about their assessment, and vice versa.

This exercise will give you a clearer picture of the talent and human resources that you already have in your team.

Complete an inventory for yourself, and ask your leadership team to do the same, and use this as the basis for a discussion about your own roles, responsibilities, skills and capabilities, and how you might leverage these moving forward. Give careful thought, as leaders, to how much time you spend on strategic/leadership tasks and how much time you spend on day-to-day operations. What do you need to step away from in order to really embrace your leadership role?

As an aside... be careful what you do with/how you store or file this information. ALWAYS ensure that you are complying with data protection legislation around personal information!

Where are they all?

As your company grows, you'll need to be deliberate about the structure of your business and about who reports to whom.

Focus on your current structure for a minute. It may be that, back in the beginning, you set out with a plan in mind, and your current company structure makes complete sense and is efficient. At the other end of the spectrum, it may have grown organically and according to your business needs at the time, and the structure might be a bit haphazard.

Now is the time to review your current situation and devise a stable and efficient structure that will support your company growth as you scale.

With your leadership team, draw out your current company structure with reporting lines. Or you could use post-its. Either way, get a diagram of your current structure down on paper, and look closely at reporting lines.

If your company structure looks like this, with a few people reporting to you as CEO and others reporting to them, this is a good foundation.

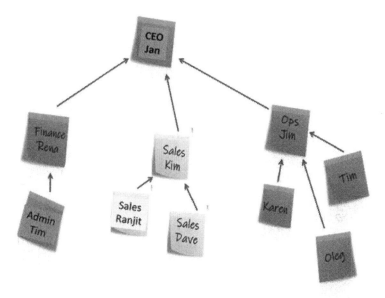

If it looks a bit more like this (below), with too many people reporting directly to you, then it's time to work out a more streamlined structure that will serve you into the future.

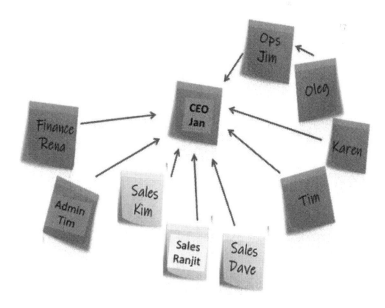

Where do they need to be and what do they need to do?

By now you'll have a clearer idea of who does exactly what in your business, and the current structure into which they fall.

Now is the time to look at your future strategy, the roles and responsibilities needed to deliver on that strategy, and define at what point they need to be brought in.

- Are there any glaring gaps in your current structure?
- How will you fill those gaps? Who needs to be in place?
- Who will they report to?
- What will their key responsibilities be?
- What's the priority, and who needs to be in place first?
- Is there anyone in your current team who could step into a leadership role, if needed?
- Will you hire people in, or outsource/contract to specialists?

Look carefully at these priorities. It may feel like the best thing to do is to hire a sales team to bring clients in, but who's supporting this internally? Who's overseeing operations, finance, HR and everything else?

A word to the wise here: plotting all this out on a large piece of paper on your boardroom table might seem unnecessary, but it's a valuable exercise, because you'll be able to physically SEE where the gaps are. One entrepreneur I was working with was pretty certain in her own mind that her hiring strategy was on point until we did this...and it became clear that her priority should switch from the current focus on building the sales team to bringing someone in at operations management level. Otherwise, she'd run the risk of being the sole line manager for over 20 staff. As CEO, this just wasn't going to work in practical terms: she was already getting bogged down in day-to-day operations rather than focusing on growing the business.

One you have a clearer idea of who you need to have on board as you move forward, look closely at your existing team.

- Who might grow into one of these new roles?
- What training and support will they need?
- Who's willing to learn, and take on a fuller role?

- Who joined the company with the expectation of building their role as the business grew?

- What's the best structure for what you need to deliver in the next 12-18 months and beyond?

- Where do sensible 'lines of command' and reporting structures fall?

- And crucially...how will you manage and prioritise your budgets etc to be able to bring people on board?

YOU as the leader

Whilst we're looking at the people you'll be bringing into your business here, take a good look at yourself. How are you going to lead this larger team of people? How will you delegate responsibility, clearly communicate strategy and goals and provide an environment in which your team can work well?

It's probably not stretching the truth too much to say that if you don't grow and change, your business won't either, so look closely at where you sit with all this.

If you're really someone who feels that they aren't a 'people person' or that they don't do the 'touchy-feely stuff', rest assured that this is actually a key part of your business. If you don't fancy taking on the task of leading and role modelling the people stuff, make sure there's someone in your business who can and will.

Referring back to the 'Pea #1: Personal' section from time to time will help to ensure that you remain true to your own values and aspirations as you grow your business, and that you're clear on your current capabilities, what you need to learn in this area, and what you should let go of.

Focus on YOU in your CEO role:

- What actually ARE your roles and responsibilities, moving forward?

- What are you currently doing that you can delegate in order to create the space to work on your business rather than in it?

- Where do you need to focus more?

- Which aspects of the people side of your business come easily to you?

- Which aspects do you find more challenging... that you might try to avoid?

Think also about your leadership team.

How must they operate as they take the lead in managing different areas of your business, whilst retaining a clear overall vision, and working as a team themselves?

What do they – like you – also need to 'learn, leverage or leave'?

CHAPTER SUMMARY:

- Your business structure must change as you grow.
- You and your leadership team must focus on high-level activities, and trust others to deliver on your strategy.
- You need a clear understanding of your current structure and everyone's roles and responsibilities as well as an idea of what your structure needs to be in five years' time (or whatever time frame you've chosen to work with) in order to develop your people strategy.
- Taking a 'people inventory' will allow you to see who might be developed into future roles, and who is best suited to stay where they currently are.
- Consider yourself and your leadership team in all of this, too.

NOTES:

_____

_____

_____

_____

_____

_____

_____

_____

_____

_____

_____

_____

_____

_____

_____

_____

_____

_____

_____

CHAPTER 8

DELIVERING RESULTS
THROUGH OTHER PEOPLE

As your business grows, ALL the leaders within it, from first line managers to your leadership team, will have to know how to deliver results through other people. It's something to start building into your business ecosystem as early as possible, so that it becomes culturally part of what you do before it technically has to.

Setting goals that align with your strategy

In the 'Pea #2: Purpose' section, we looked at taking your vision, mission, goals and longer-term plans and priorities and breaking them down into goals that each function within your business must strive towards. Here, we're taking it down to a more 'granular' level and looking at taking those functional aims and cascading them down into personal goals over the next 3 months in '321 goals' for individual team members.

Setting clear goals and managing performance is something that everyone – everyone – in a leadership role must be comfortable with, without exception.

What often happens – and the larger the organisation, the more obvious this becomes – is that at a senior level, everyone is clear on the overall strategy AND the reasons behind it. They communicate this to those on the management rung below them, but somewhere between the leadership team and the people at the coal face, the 'what' they are to do remains, but the 'why' gets lost somewhere.

Don't lose the 'why'. Ever. Everyone in your business must have a clear line of sight between what they are doing on a day-by-day basis, how this is actually contributing to business results, and what that means for everyone, including themselves. When people feel connected to something bigger than they are, they are more motivated and energetic in their activities. If, on the other hand, they are doing something "because the CEO has put it in the strategy", it's less useful to morale and motivation, and ultimately to productivity.

So, what currently happens within your business?

- How are team and individual goals currently communicated?
- How are you ensuring that those in a management position are communicating the 'why' to their teams, as well as the 'what'?
- How is progress towards goals monitored, measured and reviewed?

I'm not suggesting implementing some huge, corporate-esque appraisal system here: in the 20 years I've been working with corporates, I've not come across a single one that's entirely happy with how their own annual appraisal system works, which suggests that there's something inherently wrong with the idea in practice.

What I AM suggesting is that you're really clear on how your growth strategy translates into day-to-day activities for individual staff members, and how you and your management team keep everyone on track and pulling in the same direction.

As a basic, non-negotiable foundation:

- Everyone's goals should clearly align with your strategy...and with your overall vision and mission.
- Everyone should see and understand this.
- Progress towards goals should be managed, measured and reviewed.

Goal-setting for the team

At the risk of stating the obvious, goals and instructions are not the same thing.

A little while ago, I was running a workshop for new leaders and asked them to work in small groups. Each group was to write a clear and specific goal for one of the other teams to execute: make an aeroplane or a boat or a 'fortune teller' out of paper.

After a few minutes, their goal statements would be passed to another team to build. Finally, the planes (or whatever) would be tested and the team that had set the goal would give feedback.

This simple activity yielded some interesting results that have a clear bearing on real life.

Some assumed that their colleagues would know what to do and simply wrote, "Make a paper aeroplane." When the resulting plane didn't fly too well, the feedback was, "It was supposed to fly at least the length of the table."

How often does that happen in real life? The goal that we give people isn't the fullest expression of what we actually want them to do... and then we become disappointed when they didn't deliver what was in our heads, but remained unspoken/undocumented.

Other teams set about writing a detailed set of instructions: "Take an A4 piece of paper and fold one corner to the other side and press down. Tear off the piece at the top so that you have a square."

The executing team did end up with a 'fortune teller', but commented that they had no idea what they were making until towards the end.

Other teams wrote clear goals stating what their colleagues were to make, what the plane should look like and what it should be able to do, and then let them create something that met that brief.

My point here is this: focus on goals, not instructions (unless, of course, it's critical that the 'how' always follows the same process, and that instructions are followed exactly).

Often in the training room, I'll ask people, "Who's familiar with SMART goals?" and pretty much every hand goes up. Cheesy old SMART goals. For goodness sake, Annabelle, is this the best you can do?

Even if you don't follow them to the letter – sometimes it's simply not possible – it's worth checking that the goals you're setting follow the pattern:

Specific: Something more than the vague "make a paper aeroplane" statement. Define what success looks like clearly, and make it a bit of a stretch and a challenge for the individual. If everyone's just doing what they did last year, your business isn't moving forwards.

Measurable: What are the milestones and how will you know if you've reached them? If you're setting behavioural goals around your business values, what are the indicators that these are being met or not? (For example, if 'teamwork' is one of those values, what would someone have to actually DO to demonstrate that they are upholding this value?)

Achievable: Is the accomplishment of the goal within their control? Let's face it – unexpected things can happen, and goals often have to be revisited when external factors change. The goal should, though, be within their control and a realistic expectation. I was once told by a senior manager that I had to raise £3 million in additional funding for the organisation, with no extra budget to invest in fundraising, and just the existing members of my team...who had to continue to deliver on their day-to-day jobs, too. Ridiculous.

Relevant: Make all goals relevant to your overall business direction, and make sure that the person being given this goal sees how they're contributing to the overall business.

Time-bound: What's the deadline? What are the timescales? This is often the piece that gets missed...meaning that things simply don't happen, having become lost on someone's 'to do' list.

You might be rolling your eyes at this point at how obvious this is, but believe me, it's one of those things that we may know, but we don't necessarily execute on. Hundreds of hours delivering workshops and coaching leaders in major corporate environments indicates to me that these are things we take for granted, and which can therefore be overlooked.

Hold these things in mind as you set goals for yourself and your team. The quality and clarity of the goal you set is the yardstick by which you'll be checking for progress, so it needs to be approached thoroughly and communicated well.

The great goal cascade

Obviously enough, as the business leader, you're not setting individual goals for everybody: the leaders below you will set goals for their team members, based on the goals you set for them and their functions.

Work first with your leaders to clarify the following higher-level team/function goals, including possible barriers to achieving these (both within and outside your business).

Look closely at apparent contradictions between team goals (the marketing team wanting to invest money and the finance team wanting to save it, for example). Where's the balance? What's the priority? How will those two teams work together and communicate so that they don't start working in isolation and become rivals?

Your leaders will take those goals back to their teams and set goals with individual team members, according to their job role.

- What will each person be responsible for delivering?

- What are their priorities, according to their job role?

- What will they be measured on?

- What values/behaviours will they be measured on?

- How and when will you communicate these goals?

- How will these goals be captured and documented so you don't lose track?

- How and when will you catch up on and review their progress formally/ informally? (This does NOT mean falling into the corporate annual review system. Consider what's right for your business and your team.)

Answering these questions will give you the foundation of your early performance management system.

From strategy to individual goals

Remember the work you did in our 'Pea #2: Purpose' section to translate your overall strategic priorities into functional and/or team goals?

The same principles apply when setting individual goals. Your team members may have many tasks to undertake, but it's important that they know what key priorities they are accountable for – priorities that are actually driving your business forward, not just maintaining the status quo.

Don't just allocate goals to people: have a conversation with them. Perhaps from their grassroots position they can see challenges that you're not aware of. Maybe they have a better way of approaching something. Perhaps they'll need some specific support or resources to be able to deliver on their goals. You'll need to know all of this.

I'd recommend capturing main goals – Key Performance Indicators, to use the jargon – on an individual rolling 3-month plan (a '321 plan'), ensuring that whatever is on THIS plan lines up with what's on the overall team/function plan, which in turn lines up with your overall strategy and purpose.

NAME

Key deliverables

Key Activities

Key Measures

Remember that whatever tasks you're asking them to undertake, or results you want them to strive for, they should be backed up by your business values.

A few years ago my 80-something-year-old mum was out doing her weekly shopping and had stopped to 'fill in a questionnaire' about her gas and electricity usage. A few weeks later, she had a letter from her current provider saying 'sorry you're leaving us'. In the following days she received a letter from another company, welcoming her as a new customer.

It turned out that having completed the 'questionnaire', she was asked to sign something to confirm that she was a real person, these were her actual responses as part of the 'research', and the clipboard-holder hadn't just made her responses up.

What she'd actually signed, of course, was a commitment to sign up to a new utility provider, for which the 'researcher' was actually a salesperson.

Now, whatever values of integrity, customer focus (or whatever the trickster's company claimed to hold), clearly they were not being followed by this individual.

Task-related goals MUST be underpinned by strong values, and these behaviours must be measured.

The result of the salesperson's actions here was damage to brand reputation for the company he represented: my mum changed back to her former supplier and registered an official complaint, which was upheld.

Soft skills are often the hardest

So now everyone's clear on their goals and expected outputs, and how they relate back to broader business goals.

Your role (and that of your leadership team) from here on is to orchestrate your team and create the conditions for them to succeed. Your leaders/managers further down the business must do the same.

So now we shift our emphasis here from setting goals and so on to 'soft skills'; ironically, these are often the hardest skills to master.

Communication is the glue that holds any business together, and it's going to be critical in the way in which you work with your people. (And by that, I mean TWO-WAY communication, not just top-down communication.)

If you feel that you're not a 'touchy-feely people person', don't worry. We're not talking about group hugs and endless high-fives here; we're talking about leveraging core skills (which we all have as human beings) in order to connect with your team better, and lead them more effectively.

Key factors include:

- Know your people
- Know your 'measurables'
- Know how and when to communicate

Know your people:

How well do you and your leadership team know your people beyond their ability to contribute to your business? (How well do you know yourselves?!) Academic research shows that successful leaders are emotionally intelligent, so even if you don't feel that you are a 'people person', it's worth investing time and effort to build your skills in this area.

- How well do you know your team's strengths and weaknesses?
- Are they task-focused or people-focused?
- Do they focus on the vision and the big picture or on the data and the details?
- How does this knowledge impact how you work with and through them?
- How emotionally intelligent are you? How can you build your skills in this area?

Now, you might be saying to yourself, "I don't really care, frankly, as long as they get the work done."

Watch out for that attitude. An understanding of the people in your team, and an ability to really communicate with them, will make your people more productive and your business more profitable. It will make you a better influencer, delegator, and all-round leader.

You owe it to yourself and your business to get to grips with at least some of it... or hire someone else with preferences and skills in this area who can cover your blind spots.

Daniel Goleman, in his book, *Working with Emotional Intelligence*, highlights key factors in this area:

- Know yourself, and build your self-awareness
- Manage your emotions ('manage', please note – not 'squash' or 'ignore')
- Know how to motivate yourself
- Understand others, and their preferences, foibles and basic humanity
- Build interpersonal skills

All of these are essential leadership skills in any context or setting.

Know your measurables:

You'll have heard the saying, "What gets measured gets done", so exactly what are you measuring, how, and why? Obviously, as a leader you'll be measuring key metrics around finance, productivity and efficiency, sales and marketing, employee satisfaction and so on – those higher-level functional goals that we've already looked at.

At this point, it's worth having a quick look back to your notes from the 'Capability' chapter in the first section, and double-checking that you aren't focused on certain metrics and not others because that's where your preference and personality lies. If you're very sales-focused, what are your process metrics? If you're completely fixated on sales but have inefficiencies in terms of delivery, you could be losing money, or leaving it on the table.

If your sole concern is building equity in the business and increasing profits at the expense of all else and you take your eye off the ball with employee satisfaction and working environment, you may start to find that your best people are leaving, or you're not attracting top talent because your culture stinks.

Whatever your performance metrics, make sure you're measuring the right things – factors that are building your business and ensuring long-term stability – and not things that you think you ought to measure because everyone else is. Once you and your team are clear on these, it becomes easier for individuals to track their own progress against their goals, and for leaders to do the same.

At an individual level, your team members must also be clear about what they're being measured on. It will help them to focus on what's really important to your business, and to establish day-to-day priorities. Don't leave them guessing – make sure you're communicating clearly.

- How sure are you that individuals know what they are responsible for delivering?

- How clearly do individual team members understand how their own goals and KPIs impact other areas of the business?

- What are the measurable outputs that you're looking for from each team/department? How clearly do individual goals tie in with these?

- When measuring behavioural goals, how are you capturing data? What behaviours indicate that someone is showing respect, for example? What would indicate that they weren't?

- How is progress towards goals being monitored and reviewed? How is it being supported and encouraged?

- How are values and behavioural standards being communicated, role modelled and maintained?

Years ago I heard this story. I'm not sure if it's true or not, but it's a good one anyway. Apparently, in days of yore when sailors were venturing off around the world on daring expeditions of discovery in search of new lands, they would look for signs of 'land ahoy'.

Before they could see the cloud formations that typically indicate that land is ahead, they would notice debris in the water – sticks and leaves. Signs of solid ground.

Once they saw the sticks and leaves floating in the sea, they would know they were heading in the right direction – landfall was not far off.

Even if the story is nonsense (sailors among you – please don't write in to correct me), it's a useful metaphor: what are the 'sticks and leaves' that will indicate to your team that they're heading in the right direction?

Know when and how to communicate:

Communication is the glue that holds any business together. The subject area warrants an entire library to even begin to cover it adequately, so I'm just going to focus on a few key points here that are relevant to managing team performance.

Pretty much every business I've ever worked with, whatever its size and wherever in the world it is, shares this trait: when I ask people to rate themselves as communicators on a scale of 1-10, the vast majority will put themselves at a 6 or above. Some recognise that they should make more of an effort, but they all see themselves as at least adequate in this regard.

When I ask what are some of the key challenges within the business as a whole, guess what comes up? You guessed it – communication. That thing that everyone thinks they're pretty good at.

The underlying moral of the story is this: as in so many things, there's a massive difference between what we'd like to think we do, what we know we should do...and what we actually do. And when it comes to communicating, we could ALL do better.

One of the common excuses for not communicating is "I don't have the time." Which is, of course, the biggest excuse for not doing something anywhere in the history of the world. What this actually means is that communication isn't a priority, and as your business grows, this is a dangerous error.

MAKE time to speak to your leadership team to gauge progress, and ensure that function/team leaders are communicating with their team (properly communicating, and gathering information as well as relaying it).

Invest time in coaching them towards success, and in giving them feedback – positive where they're doing well and corrective where they're missing the mark.

Lack of communication costs your business money, so invest time in getting it right.

- How often do you meet your management team to track progress and iron out conflicts, challenges and issues?
- How do they pass on information from these meetings to their teams?
- How do you gather information from team members and ensure it gets passed back up the line?

- How are key messages communicated? (Clue: this will involve more than a statement emailed to everyone in the company.)

- How often do review conversations take place, ensuring that team members are on track to deliver the strategy – formally and informally?

- What systems and infrastructure support your internal communications and performance management?

Communication. It really IS the glue holding your business – and your people – together, and it's something everyone should be conscious of.

CHAPTER SUMMARY:

- Everyone's goals should clearly align with your strategy...and with your overall vision and mission.

- Everyone should see and understand this, and be clear on their personal role in delivering the strategy.

- Strategy and goal setting should be kept as clear and straightforward as possible.

- Over-complicating things leads to confusion, which leads to goals being missed and strategy not being met.

- Know your people, know your measurables, and know when and how to communicate.

NOTES:

PEA # 4

PROCESS

"Excellence is a continuous process and not an accident."

APJ Abdul Kalam

CHAPTER 9

YOU CAN'T SCALE WITHOUT...

Processes are one of those things that divide the room – one half claps their hands in glee at the prospect of mapping out and analysing logical, sequential behaviours and actions, whilst the other half hangs their head in gloom at what they see as a boring curb on their creative and spontaneous approach.

The stark fact of the matter is that without robust, repeatable processes and systems, your business isn't scalable. However, before the logical sequential thinkers sink back too comfortably into their seats, there's a people side to all this that is often missed.

PROCESS THINKING

If you have weak processes but motivated people, they will get things done. If you have strong processes but your team isn't motivated to follow them, those processes will fail.

Another hazard is over-processing. I was speaking to a business owner recently who said that he had thousands of processes within his business. He ran a technical business, so a lot of these processes were automations of one sort or another, but one of the interesting points of our conversation was that he felt his team were good at following processes, but weren't really connected with the overall purpose of the business, which was something he wanted to address.

As with so many things, it's a balance.

Background thinking

Businesses at various stages of their growth cycle will probably have different systems in place. The immediate focus is usually on marketing and sales, because that's what's driving revenue generation and the lifeblood of your business, so you may well have sound systems in place for this, and for related finance processes like invoicing.

As your business grows, though, you WILL need more than that in order to scale sustainably and efficiently.

Our starting point, then, is where your processes are now, and consideration of this involves a fair amount of soul-searching and brutal honesty. It will involve rummaging around and actively checking exactly what's going on, as opposed to giving it your best guess, or your overall impression based on what you see from your leadership position.

- What processes do you currently have? How well are they documented and followed?

I was working with someone recently who had little in the way of processes for hiring or managing team performance. As a very results-driven individual, his request was for "a set of processes that people can follow." That would have been easy enough, but pretty pointless if they remained mere documents in a folder somewhere, not followed or acted upon.

The presence of procedures, however well-documented they might be, is irrelevant if they are not followed.

- Who's involved in each of your processes? Who's impacted by them? Who designs them?

These three groups of people must talk to each other. This doesn't mean a free-for-all where everyone and their dog chips in and has an equal say in trying to create something, though. That would be inefficient and ineffective in the long run. It simply means including the right people in the discussion at some level, so that nothing important gets missed.

I recently came across a marketing executive who had done a good deal of work for his company. He had decided that the sales team needed a new CRM system, as a formalised method of categorising and tracking sales leads. He went as far as recommending some specific systems in which the company should invest, but unfortunately, he'd not spoken about this with the sales team who'd actually be using the system. Unsurprisingly, they weren't too happy. Why? It was a good system and process to advocate. It would benefit the business, and ultimately (once they'd got to grips with it) would make life easier for the sales team – so what was their problem?

Human nature kicked in, that's what. It was change. They'd not been consulted on what they would want out of a new CRM system. They didn't really get on with the marketing team anyway, so why would they do anything that they suggested?

Investment in a costly CRM system without asking end users what they need, and explaining the rationale for the change, is setting up trouble for later on, when people don't use the new process and system...and then blame that process or system for not working.

By way of another example, there used to be a programme on TV where a senior member of a company's board would don a disguise and go and work amongst their front-line staff, to see what really went on at the coalface.

In one episode, the Finance Director of a car manufacturer (the Managing Director was too well-known and would have been recognised) was working alongside a valet in one of their larger showrooms.

Senior management had decided that a bonus for being a high-value customer was that your car would be valeted at no extra charge when it was brought in for a service. Accordingly, the leadership team devising this special offer had drawn up a checklist of what this valeting service was to include: hosing down wheel arches, vacuuming seats and the rest of it. They'd also allocated specific times during which these individual tasks were to be completed.

As the FD worked alongside the valet, he struggled to keep up. "How on Earth do you do it in the time?" he asked.

"We don't", came the reply. "You actually can't do it properly in the time so we get it done as best we can, but sometimes we're keeping the customer waiting, because there's a queue of cars needing to be done."

Reflecting later and talking into the camera, the director commented on how that particular process was failing. "I remember the meeting where we came up with that idea", he said. "We just put an estimate of the time we thought it would take. We didn't ask anybody who actually valets the cars."

There we have it: two cautionary tales. As you analyse your current processes and start to think about how they need to change to meet the needs of your growing business, involve those who need to be involved. Don't work in a vacuum.

- How detailed do your processes need to be?

To some extent, the processes you have will be dependent on the levels of knowledge of your users. As a bit of a Luddite, I'm at the "there's a red button on the front of your computer tower. Press it. Your computer is now on" end of the spectrum. Others far more able than me will be capable of following processes that include complex instructions because they already know the basics.

Where you really DO need a process (and in some instances there are legal requirements – health and safety, for example, or your disciplinary procedure, depending on where in the world you are), bear in mind a straightforward maxim: if the process is to be repeated without error, it needs to be crystal clear.

Even if the process is being captured for the benefit of people with a good background knowledge and experience, it must be expressed in a way that someone new to the job would be able to pick up and run with on their first day.

A few years ago I was working with a manufacturing company in India, reformatting some of their process manuals into e-learning formats. Thankfully I was working with a technical expert in these things, and one who clearly understood the requirements of process documentation in that environment.

Some of the process information we received was very vague: "Move things to the side", for example. What things? Tools? Equipment? Off-cuts from the machine? Anything that's not bolted to the floor?

And to which side? And for how long?

To someone working day in and day out with a process, these things will be obvious, but someone new in a role would struggle to be sure exactly what to do. If a process is to genuinely be repeatable, there should be no margin for error.

Consider also where processes and systems need to be compatible: sales and finance, for example. The sale and the price are agreed and someone in finance sends the invoice, or it happens automatically. How are 'crossover' processes currently aligned and handed over from one person to another, or from one function to the next?

- Are your processes ones which must be followed to the letter, or is there scope for personal interpretation?

There are always going to be some processes which must be followed absolutely to the letter, to comply with the law, to avoid mistakes or accidents, and so on. There will also be processes that might be a little more flexible, of the "if this...then that" sort. Be clear in your own mind which is which, and make sure your team is also clear on when and where the process must be followed strictly and where there are margins for interpretation or creativity.

Don't be tempted to 'err on the side of caution' and make everything compulsory. A few years ago I was working with a team leader in a large organisation who 'managed' his team through a series of processes and procedures. His concern within the workshop was that his team weren't proactive and didn't tend to take initiative, and this was a source of frustration and annoyance to him. Whilst it wasn't the whole answer, the fact that his team were being trained and almost programmed to follow process and instruction was a big part of it: they weren't proactive because that wasn't a behaviour he encouraged. It wasn't part of the culture of the team. So they stuck with their comfort zone of "we do what we're told."

In this case, the leader needed coaching to turn this around. The problem wasn't his team – it was him.

- What software, hardware and other tools are you using to support your processes and systems?

Several years ago, I walked into a company (with whom I decided not to work) and noted with curiosity a huge book – rather like one of those antique family bibles – on a desk in the back office. When I asked what it was, I was told it was the 'log book'. All of the jobs were written in the left-hand column, with various other pieces of information stretching across the page. The keeper of this weighty tome was Margaret. One or two others knew her system, but it certainly wasn't accessible to all, and anyone who wanted to know what was going on had to troop downstairs to her desk to check The Log Book.

The Managing Director of this business – which was by no means unsuccessful – was of the mindset that if it had worked for the last 15 years, clearly it wasn't broken, so there was no need to fix it.

I hardly need to say that this was as far from future-proof as it's possible to be. Heaven help them if they'd ever had a fire. Or if Margaret won the lottery and left.

Consider carefully – and ask those who actually use the tools often – which of them are fit for purpose, and when you'll need to upgrade them before they start to compromise on efficiency rather than promote it.

CHAPTER SUMMARY:

- Capture your processes, systems and measures as they are...not as you'd like to think they are.
- Consult those who actually use the processes.
- Processes are only efficient if people design, use and improve them properly.
- The tools that support your processes must be fit for the purpose.

NOTES:

CHAPTER 10

THE PROCESS SIDE OF PROCESS

Processes can be complex, and even as a fairly random thinker myself, I know that it's best to approach them methodically and accurately. There is space for creativity when it comes to process improvement, but in general, this is an area where disciplined thought is a must.

Capturing what already exists

First of all, there will be nuances depending on whether you're capturing existing processes, designing them from scratch or improving them. As always, having a really clear idea of exactly what's going on NOW is going to enable you to focus your efforts on improving what needs to be improved.

A starting point here is to consider what processes and systems are currently in place. This will be different, to an extent, from business to business, but typical business processes include:

- Marketing
- Sales
- Finance (reporting, invoicing, etc).
- HR
- Service Delivery
- Product Development
- Management
- Communication

Which of these do you have, and which do you need?

Place aside for the moment those processes which you don't yet have – we'll come back to those later. Start with processes that you already have.

I'd recommend focusing your attention first on those areas where you have an inkling that there might be room for improvement. This doesn't mean overlooking those areas which you sense might be working well. It's simply a matter of prioritising.

Pick a process, and go through it meticulously, accurately, and above all, honestly. Ask the people who actually work with the process regularly to be involved in this: it's 'their' process after all, and as we'll see in our next chapter, gaining your team's involvement and 'buy-in' to your processes is essential.

What are the actual steps involved? What actually happens, even if it's not what's supposed to happen? Brutal honesty is required here. If the information isn't captured accurately, there's almost no point in bothering at all, because you'll end up with an 'all clear' signal whether or not this is actually the case. (Remember those business values in our 'Pea #2: Purpose' section? Were honesty and openness amongst them?!)

Ensure that your people are telling you what's actually going on, not what they think you want to hear.

Look at any discrepancies between what's meant to happen, as documented in your operating manual, and what's actually happening, and investigate these. Where the process isn't followed, or falls down at any point, look for patterns as to why or how. Is the process inefficient, so people are taking shortcuts? Are there issues with the software or tools you're using? Don't be quick to assume the answers – be thorough.

When you're analysing and measuring how effective your processes are, it's important to be clear what you're actually measuring against. There might be legal requirements or standards that customers or clients expect, or it might be your own notions of excellence (in which case, make sure they are realistic).

There's no point in analysing and measuring for the sake of it. Don't lose sight of the big picture here.

- How are your processes – and the stages within them – actually adding value to your business?

- Are they robust enough to support your business as it scales up?

- Do they support your team in the delivery of their objectives, in alignment with the overall strategy?

- Who 'owns' or takes responsibility for each process? Where does ownership of the process change hands? (For example, marketing processes will pass to the sales team, and once the sale is made, to the service delivery team.) Where exactly does it change hands and how smooth is the transition? What happens at that point?

One of the things I've noticed is that when we look at the lifecycle of an employee, from their very first interaction with the company through a job advert or recruitment company, through their interview, onboarding, and performance management, right until they leave the company through retirement, resignation, redundancy, or being fired... the whole process is owned by the HR function.

When we look at the customer lifecycle, though, it typically starts with the marketing team, and the various outreach messages it's delivering, then moves on to the sales team who seal the deal, and once the sale has been made, on to the service or product delivery team. If things don't go well, a complaints team might have to pick up the pieces.

Unfortunately, when processes dovetail in this way, the ball is often dropped at the handover point, which is why it's vital to look closely at this. Do the processes align? Do the people involved recognise that the quality of what they pass on is crucial – not just to the person being passed owner-ship of that part of the process – but to the business as a whole?

The long and short of it is that they must.

Give careful thought as to who is impacted by the process at each stage, and what exactly is happening at the handover points.

Consider also the tools that you're using to support your process. If you've had them in place for a while, are they still relevant and efficient, or is it a matter of 'mend and make do'? It's actually surprising how many companies – large ones as well as small – continue in a makeshift way with some of their processes until they're creaking at the joints and in danger of falling to pieces, at which point it can be costly to fix them and implement something that's fit for purpose and a little more future-proof.

Budgets will come into play, obviously – but is it time to invest in upgrades now in order to save you time and money in the future?

Map out your processes. Assign names next to those elements which have specific 'owners' and look for gaps. Make a note of the tools used at each point.

Capture it as it is, and look for patterns, gaps, what's working well, and what isn't. Document the lot.

Improving current processes

If you've had a thorough look at your processes with your team, you should have an idea of areas where improvement is needed. Such improvement may be required because it's not working as well as it might right now, or because the process is expected to soon be reaching a limit. Whilst it might do for now, it's coming up to its sell-by date, and retooling is necessary if the process is to support the delivery of your future strategy.

Look at your overall strategy, and consider not just what you have now, but what's needed in the coming months and years.

- Where do your current processes support your future growth, and where do they need to be improved, or even redesigned from scratch?

- Where is there currently waste, inefficiency or a bottleneck?

- Where is there duplication of efforts, or a variety of ways of doing the same thing (where one would be best)?

- What improvements are needed in tools, software or automation in order to deliver on the strategy?

Before diving in to streamline things to within an inch of their life, pause for a moment and think about your business in broader terms. Where can (or will) you NOT make sacrifices to process improvement?

Health and safety is a case in point here: not only is good practice required by law, but ensuring the physical safety of staff is the right and decent thing to do and cannot be compromised. It may also be that process improvements in the name of efficiency are somehow at odds with your brand, or the quality of your product or service. A bespoke tailoring service, for example, could be far more efficient by cutting out numerous steps in its own processes, but those steps are part of its unique proposition, and are exactly what the customer is paying for.

On the other hand, it can be tempting to add stages to your processes, and again it's important to consider the overall impact of these. One thing that seems to be prevalent among online 'gurus' is an 'application process' for working with them. It's probably designed to make them look terribly busy and important and as though there's a queue of people lining the street to work with them. For me, though, it's an unnecessary step and one I won't take. I think to myself, "Look – do you want to talk to me or not?"

On the service delivery side, I was working with someone recently who started to 'throw in a few extras' to his service delivery, and rather than being one-offs, they were starting to become part of the overall process. The thing was, whilst it was a nice-to-have from a customer point of view, it wasn't adding particular value from their perspective, and it was costing him time and effort (and therefore money). The added element of process wasn't worth it.

If you add steps to your process, be aware of the overall impact of doing so.

Process improvement should not come at the expense of another important aspect of your business, and should be something that your future business needs, so make the call and stick to it.

The process of process improvement, if you will, looks a little like this:

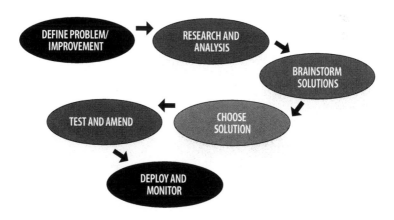

Define the problem or the improvement needed:

There's a balance here between "if it ain't broke, don't fix it" and recognising that, even if it "ain't broke", it could still be better, or perhaps even that it needs to be better to support your future strategy. Think of that giant log book on Margaret's desk.

What DOES your future business need, and what's the gap between that future process, and what's going on now?

Look again at your strategy and your overall business aspirations for the next few years. What processes, systems and tools will your future business need in order to run efficiently and genuinely scale up?

What are the priorities, and how will you budget and plan for them?

Research and analyse:

This research and analysis piece may involve revisiting the work you've already done to capture your existing process to scrutinise certain aspects. Or it might be something else – current best practice, advances in your sector or in the tools or software that you're using, what your competitors are doing, or what your customers are really looking for. Consider carefully what needs further investigation.

Sometimes pinpointing what the actual issue is can be a bit like fixing a leak in your house: you can see that there's a damp patch on the wall, but you're not sure what's causing it. Simply re-plastering the wall and painting over it won't work.

So it is with process improvements. The improvement might actually be needed in an area where the problem isn't showing up.

A few years ago I was working with an engineering company where time and money was being lost – as well as customer goodwill – because engineers would frequently turn up on site with the wrong piece of kit or not quite the right part or tool, and have to head back to HQ to find the correct bits and pieces before actually starting the work.

Whilst these people were bearing the brunt of customer complaints, on analysis, it transpired that one of the source issues was that the customer accounts team handling incoming calls were not asking specific enough questions about what the client actually needed.

The result of this was that only general rather than specific information was being gathered. Engineers were having to chase up for more information and the customer accounts team didn't want to bother the client again on the same issue, so engineers would usually just give it their best guess on the basis of the information they received...and sometimes they got it wrong.

The challenge in addressing this was that the people who were unwittingly causing the problem weren't directly affected by the problem, so motivation to change was a key issue.

Brainstorm ideas:

It stands to reason that when you're coming up with ideas for fixing or improving a process, you consult people who are affected by the process as well as those who actually work with it. I'd also suggest including a couple of people who have nothing to do with it whatsoever, because from their external position, they might be able to see something that those who are close to the process have missed, and they might be able to bring insights and ideas from their own area of expertise.

A diversity of experience, background and opinions always makes for a much more useful brainstorming session than the usual suspects sitting round a table with a pile of post-it notes, calling out random ideas.

There are many different methods of brainstorming. There must be at least a dozen that I use in workshops and seminars. Choose a method that you like, and perhaps one or two that are new, just to vary things and to stimulate fresh thinking.

Remember when you're brainstorming that you're looking to generate as many ideas as possible at this stage, so don't be tempted to rule any out, however off-the-wall they might seem. Now is the time for the creative brain to spring into action – the 'editor' brain will be called upon in a minute.

Choose a solution:

In fact, this is where your editor brain – the logical analysis – kicks in, as you look closely at the ideas you've come up with and assess their viability as practical solutions or improvements, consider costs and benefits, assess the wider impact of changes and so on.

The key point is to choose a way forward, and to plan implementation of that solution, including any milestones or those 'sticks and leaves' indicators that will tell you that you're heading in the right direction.

I'm hoping it goes without saying by now, but this is not something to plough through alone. Involve others – people who can offer alternative perspectives and input to the conversation, and who can offer their thoughts as to the practicalities of the implementation plan.

A past head teacher at my kids' school (who wasn't too popular with either staff or students) once said, "I know that I've made a good decision because I look at all the options carefully so I know I've made the right one." Unfortunately, she didn't seem to involve anyone else in her decision-making process, and with her limited perspective, she wasn't always making the right decision (no one is that infallible). The staff were less inclined to wholeheartedly put these decisions into practice since they didn't feel listened to.

Don't fall into the trap of thinking this is something you can do alone (indeed, that growing a business is something you can do alone). It really isn't.

Test and amend:

Keeping a close eye on those milestones and indicators which you've identified in your planning stage, and being absolutely honest about whether or not the chosen intervention is actually working or not, are key. Now is not the time for egos to come into play, as the originators of ideas cling fast to them in the face of required changes (something I've seen a few times in the past).

Testing and amending must obviously keep in mind the starting point of the whole exercise: the solution to a problem or the improvement of the process in some way. There's no point in change for change's sake, so be clear about what your original objectives were, and about the measurements and indicators that are telling you whether your endeavours have been successful.

The benchmarks you're measuring against should be the ones you identified when you planned out how you'd implement your ideas. Don't lose sight of these.

Deploy and monitor:

Once you've settled on a way forward, perhaps after a few trials or tests and amendments, it's time to set the new, improved process as 'business as usual'.

- Who needs to know about this? Users of the process, as well as those impacted?

- Where does process documentation need to be updated and filed?

- Who's going to monitor the new process to ensure that the benefits continue, and make any necessary tweaks moving forward?

- When will the process be reviewed, and by whom?

Processes and systems are never just 'set it and forget it': in order to maintain efficiency, consistent monitoring will be needed.

Designing a process from scratch

You might find that you're designing certain processes from a standing start – possibly things that you've improvised around since starting up but which now need a more formal structure around them so that they can be duplicated and scaled.

As with all process management design and improvement, this isn't a one-person task: speak to the people who will be working with the process and are impacted by it as part of your discussions.

Here's an outline structure of this process-related process:

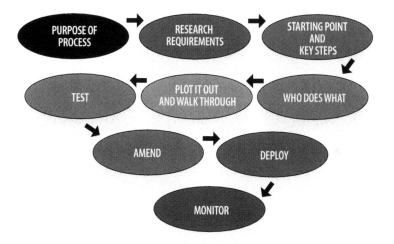

Purpose of the new process:

There's no point in creating processes for the sake of it, so the first thing to consider is what actually needs a documented process, and why.

- What does it need to achieve for you, your team and your business?

- How is it helping support your strategy and drive your business growth?

- How important is it that everyone follows one process and does the same thing in the same way?

- Are there legal requirements or compliance standards that must be followed?

- Is it just more efficient if there's a set method for doing something, so that if someone's ill or on holiday, another member of the team can fill in for them?

- Does the addition of a properly documented process add to the value of your business, or save time and money?

Whilst it's true that most areas of a business will benefit from clear and robust process management, there will always be areas where the process is more fluid than concrete. For example, the sales process I follow for larger clients involves a meeting or two, drafting a proposal, and negotiations on project specifics following the acceptance of that proposal.

Whilst I can document key phases in the process, there are elements which require experience to tackle – the negotiation aspect, for example, or the creative input to the proposal, which will differ from client to client depending on their needs.

If you're looking to devise an online sales funnel, on the other hand, the entire process will be mapped out in great detail, automated, and every client will follow the same route.

Research the requirements:

What requirements are needed to ensure the new process's success? Do you need support from external experts (HR, finance)? Or perhaps new tools or software?

As this is a new process you're designing, having an idea of what will actually be needed in order for it to function effectively is important; external advice might well be useful here. True, there will be a certain amount that you'll figure out and clarify along the way, but make sure that you're capturing this type of data and information.

You'll also need to be clear about factors like legal requirements or other external factors that will impact the process you're designing: areas of employment law, for example, that you'll need to weave into your hiring process, or reporting procedures that may need to tie in with your client's.

You should also look at the practical parameters – is there a specific timeframe in which the process must be completed, for example, or other processes and systems within your business with which it must fit? If so, keep these clearly in mind.

Years ago I was running a workshop in a school. The kids had been tasked with working in teams to build a bridge out of spaghetti that was strong enough to support a 1kg bag of sugar once it was built.

One team in particular worked out what the bridge should look like, how big it should be, and what each person would be working on before they came together at the end and pulled it all together.

What went wrong after this promising initial stage was this: each team member worked on their own to build their bit of the bridge. When they brought the bits together at the end, it simply did not fit together – it didn't even stand up on its own, let alone support the bag of sugar.

Don't make this mistake when designing your processes. Identify your requirements and communicate with each other as you move forward to ensure that you're all still on the same page, and that each element of the process actually comes together as a whole.

Starting point and key steps:

Where DOES the process start, and what are the key steps? If you're designing a process that is going to be followed by your team in the coming months, or form the basis of some aspect of your growth plans, it's important that it's focused on achieving clear objectives, and not too influenced by the personal preferences of whoever is currently carrying out the process in an informal way.

Are the key steps all necessary? Do they add value? At the risk of being repetitive, involve other people here – they may see value in steps that you think are unnecessary, or vice versa.

The starting point and key steps that you identify must be genuinely part of a repeatable process, not just an unworkable theory that no one can actually follow (remember that valeting example!). Whilst you're going to be testing the process before making it 'business as usual' and ironing out any creases at that point, the more practical thinking that takes place at this stage, the less time you'll waste at the testing stage.

Who does what:

The new process might be something that one person or team undertakes from start to finish, or it might be one where different people or teams are involved.

- Where are the handover points, and what exactly is being passed over?

- Who is involved, and who is impacted at each stage?
- Are there people who 'feed in' to the process by providing information, resources or something else?
- How will you communicate with them to ensure that they understand their impact on the process as a whole, its objectives and outputs?

Remember to look beyond those who are actually hands-on users of the process in the design phase. For the finished process to work properly, those impacted by it, even indirectly, must be involved in the discussion at some level.

Plot it out and walk it through:

With a brand new process, plotting it out, documenting the stages in a flow chart, and going through it meticulously will help catch any missed steps. Scenario planning of this sort is always going to be important in identifying in advance aspects of the process which might prove tricky or challenging, and preparing counter-measures to deal with these before testing it all out in real life.

Although you've already documented what you think the key steps are, you might find in practice that there's a different order to the steps, that some aren't necessary, that others need to be brought in, that contingencies need to be in place and so on. It might seem like overkill, but if your process is to be robust enough to be replicated within your business, and repeatable enough to be the foundation for your scale-up, then time and effort invested here are well spent.

Again (yes, I'm saying it again), involve people who will be impacted by the process as well as those who are actually working with it day to day. The inclusion of diverse perspectives will ensure that more potential stumbling blocks are identified in advance, and can be planned for.

Test and amend, deploy and monitor:

These final stages follow the same principles as if you'd improved an existing process. Once again, the key points are to be mindful of the original purpose and success measures of the process, and once you've settled on a workable, duplicable process, to ensure that it becomes business as usual.

The mere existence of processes, operating manuals and flow charts, however, do not a system make. As we'll see in the next chapter, the way in which people follow and interact with these processes will make or break them.

And it's the people side of processes that businesses often forget.

CHAPTER SUMMARY:

- Be clear on what needs a process and why.
- Know and communicate which processes must be followed to the letter, and where there is room for interpretation and creativity.
- There's a step-by-step process for process improvement and for designing a process from scratch.
- Involve those who will be using the process at every stage.

NOTES:

CHAPTER 11

THE PEOPLE SIDE OF PROCESS

One of the factors that businesses often miss is that processes need people in order to function: people to design them in the first place, people to actually follow them, and people to actively look for opportunities to improve them and fix them where necessary.

This behavioural side of process is quite literally make or break: get it wrong and miss its significance and you'll end up wasting a fortune over the years fixing and upgrading processes, when actually what's needed is an understanding of the people side of it all. Even if you have a fully automated process as part of your digital market sales funnel, or in a factory, you'll still need human beings to oversee and monitor it, and ensure that it continues to be fit for purpose.

And those human beings need to understand why the process is important and have bought in to following and improving it. Knowing that the process exists and the steps that it involves is simply not enough.

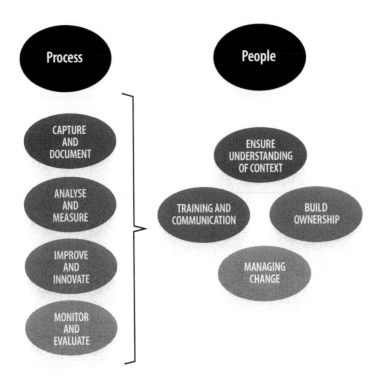

Understanding context

One of the questions that people should generally ask more often in a business context is, "Why are we doing this?" Even if processes have become so much a part of your day-to-day activities that you hardly notice they're there – perhaps even more so in this case – it's important that everyone is aware of the purpose of a particular process, why it exists and why their input is important.

This last part is crucial: if people underestimate their own importance in the process, they may start to cut corners, which in turn will have an impact elsewhere.

The old wartime song by Thompson and Heneker about a factory worker sort of sums it up:

"I can't pretend to be a great celebrity

But still I'm quite important in my way.

The job I have to do may not sound much to you

But all the same I'm very proud to say:

I'm the girl that makes the thing that drills the hole

That holds the ring that drives the rod

That turns the knob...

That works the thing-ummy-bob!"

That 'thing-ummy-bob' in this case was some technical piece of equipment that was essentially important to the war effort, and the girl is performing a vital role in its manufacture, however small it might appear to be to the casual observer.

Thoughtless throwaway comments like, "It's just the way we've always done things" or "That's the way the CEO wants it done" are dangerous. People will undervalue the process and there's a higher chance that people will be going through the motions because they have to, rather than being particularly mindful about what they're doing, or why.

Whilst it's tempting to think, "So what – as long as they follow the process, who cares?" it's important to consider more deeply the sort of culture that you want your future business to have (something that we'll be looking at in our final 'Pea #5: Paradigms' section). Do you want one where people follow processes like automatons and do what they're told, or one where people are genuinely contributing their talents and ideas to your business?

Where you're making changes to an existing process, or putting one in place where currently nothing formal exists, it's crucial that everyone understands why this is being done. Given that human beings are notoriously poor at handling change, understanding 'why' might not immediately get everyone on board with the changes, but it will certainly help.

Not explaining the context or rationale, or assuming the people will 'just know' why they're being asked to do something leaves the door wide open for them to put their own interpretations in place, and these might not be helpful.

I was hosting a session a few years ago for the UK directors of a large global corporate. Their USA headquarters had looked closely at their performance management system and reached the unhappy conclusion that while everyone was grading themselves and their teams as 'high performing' employees in the appraisal process (an impossible statistic where nearly 50% of staff thought that they were among the top 10% of performers), their actual performance as a business compared to competitors in their sector didn't reflect this. A culture was developing where people were becoming complacent about how good they were, and this simply wasn't being backed up by the overall business results.

As part of the push to address this, the CEO and his senior team had reviewed the performance management system, and were implementing a new process for reviewing and evaluating staff performance.

Logical though this step was, the rank and file were not happy that their grading (and possibly their bonus) was likely to go from "aren't you wonderful" to "actually, you're pretty ordinary"... or worse.

I found myself, if truth be told, less of a 'host' at the event to outline the new procedure to the UK directors, and more of a 'referee' between those for and against the new process.

In a seminar with 100 of their UK business leaders, one of the senior managers said what many others were thinking: "This is HR, isn't it? HR just creating jobs for themselves!"

It was a ridiculous assertion, and not one that I was going to leave unchallenged.

"OK", I said. "Give me an example of a company that you know – anyone at all – who, in these tricky economic times, is making up processes just for the sake of keeping people in jobs. Don't hold back – shout them out!"

Needless to say, there was an uncomfortable silence from the floor.

"Can we at least accept", I continued, "that the CEO didn't wake up one morning and think, 'I KNOW how I can REALLY annoy everyone and waste time and money', but that these measures have been put in place following a considerable amount of discussion and research into best practices because it's believed that this is what's best for the business at this time?"

There were murmurs of assent (thank goodness).

The point here is that even at the UK senior management level, people who hadn't been involved in the decision-making process (and let's face it, not everyone can be all of the time) felt that processes were being imposed on them, and they hadn't really been told why – they'd just been told, "This is what we're doing now."

We looked at this when we covered goal setting earlier. The context and the reasons why are important, and must be communicated.

As well as explaining how a new or improved process will work, you need to explain the reasons behind process capture, improvement and design, in terms of:

- Why things need to be improved
- The danger of NOT improving or installing processes
- What the future will be like with these new processes in place
- What the benefits will be to the business, to the team...and crucially, to them as individuals.

Just to reinforce that last point, it's absolutely crucial that the change is communicated in a way that recognises people as individuals. So often I see grandiose statements about how proposed changes will benefit the business and shareholders, and the unspoken question in everyone's minds is, "Marvellous – but what about me?!"

What ARE the personal benefits of the new process or system? Will it make their working day easier? Will it save them time? Will it protect the business as a whole, and therefore their future employment? What?

Make sure you're being honest here: stressing the benefits might be tricky if a process is being put in place that's going to see them out of a job. If this is the case, what can be done to acknowledge this and help them move forward to the next stage of their careers, either within your business or outside it? People will often step outside of their own personal concerns if they are given the space and conditions to do so.

In all aspects of this people side of process, communication is both the glue that keeps the team together and the oil that keeps things running smoothly; its importance can't be overstated. Designing the process can sometimes be the easy part. Overcoming issues of confidence or fear around the process can be a different ballgame altogether.

Looking at how your team currently works with your processes, consider the following:

- Do people skip bits of the process? Why?
- How well do you think people currently understand why all the steps in the process exist? What's telling you this?
- How prepared are people to work outside the process in an emergency? How well do they know what constitutes an emergency?

- Where do conflicts between teams or functions exist in the process?
- How are these conflicts discussed and resolved?

Establishing ownership

This might sound like corporate jargon – and perhaps it is – but the point here is that your team should feel like the process is theirs, and not just something that they've been told to do, or that has been imposed on them.

If they 'own' it, they are responsible for it, and more likely to look after it and respect it.

Years ago I used to commute by train into Glasgow, and just before the train pulled into Central Station, we'd pass a small industrial estate. One of the walls close to the railway track was covered in graffiti of that artless sort where people have just scribbled their names or drawn something obscene before the security guards chased them off.

One day, though, the journey into town revealed something different: the entire wall had been covered with street art featuring a colour palette of mainly black, white and purple, and some innovative designs around a particular theme.

That painting is still on the wall, and no one has come and scribbled over the top of it. It's 'owned' by someone who, instead of being a problem, was drawn into being part of the solution, and that eyesore graffiti is a thing of the past.

Involvement builds ownership, and ownership is powerful. It means that someone else other than you is driving the process forward, and ensuring that it stays true to your business objectives and strategy. As you grow your business, this is going to be increasingly important, because it's not the best use of your time or energy to police processes or enforce compliance.

Some practical questions to consider:

- How will you involve your wider team in the capture, improvement and design of processes?
- How will you encourage your team to report issues/problems with processes, systems, tools and measures?
- How will you encourage them to make suggestions for improvement?
- How will you recognise and reward good ideas?
- How will your leadership team build a culture of process improvement?

Training

Once you've designed a new process, or documented an existing one, you'll need to make sure that everyone is following it correctly. Where you have 'early adopters' or advocates for the new process, you can leverage their enthusiasm here, to draw others along with them.

When people are being trained on a new or improved process, it's important that these factors we've just covered are all part of it – the 'why' and the 'who', as well as the 'what' and 'how'. It's also crucial that, where a process is handled by a few different people, each one is aware of how their elements of the process impact other people, and therefore the business.

If people understand the rationale behind the process and can see the benefit of it, they're more likely to follow it... which is why we've just considered some questions around that very point. If you don't train people on the 'why', they're likely to interpret the process in their own way and do their own thing. People are a little bit like water in this respect – they will take the easiest route if there's no clear reason to do otherwise.

Someone who has to pass weekly figures on to a colleague in a different department who'll report to management on those figures needs to know the full context of what they're doing, and what they're contributing to. Otherwise there's a risk – especially as your business grows – that things will start to fall through the cracks at those handover points as people think, "I've done my bit – it's not my problem anymore."

I've written and delivered literally hundreds of training programmes over the years, and though the temptation is to take people through the process from start to finish, that's usually not the best way to make sure that they really 'get it'.

Three key points that will help are these:

1) First, be clear what you actually want them to know and be able to do with the process. Will they be required to actually work with it day to day, or simply to have enough knowledge about it to step in if required? Perhaps all they need is a basic understanding of it from a distance. What do they need to know, what do they need to do, and what do they need to feel (confident about using the process, for example, or convinced of its importance)?

Be clear also about whether the process must be followed to the letter, or whether it's flexible enough for them to go their own way a little at certain points.

2) As you plan your training, break the process into chunks and focus on a section at a time, building up knowledge and testing practical skills as you go.

If you give people a list of fifteen things to remember, they'll probably remember the first one or two, the last one or two, and perhaps something that stood out for them in the middle of the list. It's the way that memory seems to work, and it holds true for your training workshop. If you work relentlessly through from start to finish, the same will happen: your team will remember the first few elements, the last couple of things that you told them, and one or two points in between. Not particularly useful if you want someone to have a thorough and comprehensive knowledge of something.

Your best bet is to break it up and make it interesting – include visuals, questions, mini-tests, hands-on sessions – anything that will build knowledge, understanding and skills. Bombard them with a death-by-PowerPoint lecture at your peril.

3) Remember to highlight the benefits of the new process and the reason for installing it in the first place, for them as individuals as well as for the business as a whole. "What's in it for me?" is often a turning point in situations of influencing and persuading people to start doing something new.

As the new process is implemented, highlight successes so that your team can see that it's achieving its original purpose, adding value to the business, and making people's work lives easier. Seeing that it's actually working will help to ensure that it becomes a valued part of 'business as usual'.

Ongoing process improvement

I've said before that an "If it ain't broke, don't fix it", or even a "Set it and forget it" approach to business processes will not serve you well. Part of ensuring that you don't get stuck in that rut will involve building a culture where continuous improvement is just part of how you work, not a laborious chore to be tackled when absolutely necessary.

And that culture – your Paradigms – is what we'll be looking at in our final section.

CHAPTER SUMMARY:

- Processes are only efficient if people follow them properly.
- In order to do this, people must understand why they're following the process, not just what to do.
- People must be clear when processes MUST be followed to the letter, and where there is some scope for interpretation.
- People must understand where they fit into the process, and what they are passing on to someone else.
- People should be encouraged to look for ways of improving the process.

NOTES:

_____

_____

_____

_____

_____

_____

_____

_____

_____

_____

_____

_____

_____

_____

_____

_____

_____

_____

_____

_____

PEA # 5

PARADIGMS

*"If you don't have a defined culture behind you,
you're not going to be effective at executing your strategy."*

Peggy Johnson

CHAPTER 12

PINNING IT DOWN

They say that "Culture eats strategy for breakfast" – and they're right. The underlying culture of your business – the paradigms in which you operate – might initially seem to be one of those 'nice if you have the time' or 'frosting on the cake' things that you can ignore if you want to.

Not so, for two reasons. The first is that your business will have a culture whether you like it or not, and either you're creating it…or someone else is. And that 'someone else' will be a strong character or two within your team who will become the informal leaders of your business if you aren't careful.

The second is that there's an increasing body of research which highlights that companies with a strong culture (and there are specific features that make it 'positive') are more valuable in terms of their equity than those without.

This is why we're going to spend some time looking at the paradigms in which you operate: your working environment, your workplace culture, and the business and personal values that you and your team actually live day by day.

Never be tempted to underestimate the importance of your business culture. If there's ever a battle between your culture and your strategic aims, your culture will win every single time.

DEFINING YOUR CULTURAL PARADIGMS

There's a bit of a theme here, and it's been running through this book: we have to know where we are now as well as clearly identifying where we want to go if we're to actually make the journey.

Rather than trying to map all this out yourself (and here's another theme that keeps coming up), involve your team in a workshop or discussion about your culture. They will give you a fresh perspective on what's actually going on, AND if they are involved in designing your future culture, they will buy into it more readily.

Your current culture

There are a number of culture-based questionnaires and inventories available which will help identify the sort of culture your company has, and how you can build on this as you move forward. Like most of these things, they can be incredibly useful, but they aren't absolutely essential.

What you need first and foremost is the will and determination to be brutally honest about what your culture is like here and now. There will be elements of it that are productive and positive, and elements of it that aren't, which you may want to change.

As a leader, you must bear in mind that your perception of what your business culture is like might not be the same as the viewpoint of others.

A senior manager in a finance company I was working with once argued with the results of an employee engagement survey – an anonymous questionnaire that had been completed by pretty much everyone in the building. One of the findings showed that people weren't particularly motivated at work and didn't feel supported by managers as the business was going through major changes.

"I disagree", said the senior manager. "When I walk around, I see people working hard – they all seem pretty motivated to me!"

I told the group that his comment reminded me of the deputy headmistress at my school when I was about 9 or 10 years old: she was an amble-bosomed spinster ma'am with a booming voice, and we were terrified of her. If we saw her in the distance or could hear her coming round a corner, we'd immediately pull up our socks, straighten our ties and pretend we were doing something purposeful and productive.

Years later, but on a similar theme, a friend told me that his PC at work had a 'boss coming' button on one of its time-wasting games. If you were midway through a game of solitaire or something (yes, it was that long ago), you could click this 'boss coming' icon, and a spreadsheet would appear on the screen to cover it.

Leaders don't necessarily see what's actually going on.

Even if you have a small team at the moment, their perspective on the culture may well be different from yours, and it's important to recognise that their perspective counts here. In fact, it's probably the most important one in the room.

Usually when you start talking about your culture in an open discussion, people will focus on the positives first. This is valuable, obviously, but it's also important to consider the flip side – what's NOT so useful by way of the working environment?

I used to run a workshop on company culture, and one of the things I'd ask delegates to do was to pick a country – preferably a holiday destination – and pull together a short presentation on that country, as though they were a holiday tour rep trying to sell it to potential customers.

Unsurprisingly, there were numerous flowery descriptions of exotic locations – the food, the culture, the music, the architecture and so on.

All of which were, of course, true.

I then asked the delegates to focus on the same country, but as though they were activists highlighting and campaigning against some of the negative factors associated with that same place. Here, we had an unpleasant list of political corruption, child labour, poor health and safety – the darker side that we all know exists in every country around the world in some shape or form.

Following this, I'd ask them to consider their own company culture in the same way – the 'tourist brochure' version... and the more down-to-Earth 'Tripadvisor' version, and to be as open as possible about both.

In some cases, what had started out as a positive cultural aspect had reached a tipping point and started to become a negative factor. Streamlined processes and checklists that had boosted efficiency had got to the point where people weren't really thinking for themselves, they were just going through the motions and ticking the boxes.

In one instance, a charity that I was working with had a strong culture of being 'people-centred'. This actually referred to the remarkable way in which they worked with their clients living with disabilities, supporting them to live as full a life as possible within their communities. However, it had tipped over into an internal culture where staff were taking this 'people-centred' ethos to the extreme and arguing that they shouldn't have to use the new IT system because theirs was a 'people-centred' organisation and they didn't want to.

Openness, honesty and a variety of perspectives must be brought into the discussion from the outset, along with the recognition that too much of a good thing can become something unproductive if left unmanaged and unchecked.

Given that your culture weaves in and out of everything within your business, it can sometimes be difficult to spot – it's as though it's hidden in plain sight.

Asking yourself these questions might shed light on some of the patterns and behaviours that make up your current business culture:

- What are the positives about your current culture? What does everyone love about working at your company?

These are possibly the easiest things to flush out. People are usually keen to talk about what they value about their working culture. If they aren't, and people are struggling to say anything sincerely positive, be aware that your culture may already have started to turn sour without you being aware of it. If this is the case, now is the time to act – and the next chapter will help you.

- What are the negatives...the things that people DON'T like?

It may be that an anonymous questionnaire – rather like that employee engagement survey – might be the best way to tease out negative cultural factors. But there may be other indicators within your business. Are there things that annoy you, like swearing in the office, or speaking badly about customers? Do you have a sense that people tell you what you want to hear, rather than being completely honest? Are there areas of conflict – or ways of dealing with conflict – that keep coming up? Look closely at the behavioural patterns that you see: are they telling you something that your team isn't?

As a leader, you will have to place your ego aside when you look at this potentially uncomfortable aspect of your business, as it may well be that you've unknowingly contributed to a negative or unproductive culture. The leader who laughingly admits that they're "a control freak", the one who happily admits that they're "not a people person", or the one who "can't be bothered with processes – they cramp my style", are all sowing the seeds of something unpleasant that may well come back in time to bite them on the backside.

My friend and fellow consultant Phil tells a story of a company he worked with as an interim Operations Director. It had been acquired by new owners because of its product range and customer base, but it had a deeply toxic culture. Staff were rude about customers – even the high-level corporates – and the office environment was deeply unpleasant – aggressive, even. Staff, though, dismissed it all as "the way we do things around here."

Together with a new Managing Director, Phil was tasked with getting things back on an even keel, and resolving one or two serious issues that had come to light... but the existing senior managers weren't too keen.

"What did they do when they realised you were going to tackle the big issues head on?" I asked.

"They threatened to break my legs", he replied. It turned out they had already set fire to the new Managing Director's car.

A fish rots from the head down. It's an unpleasant truth, but a truth nonetheless.

(Phil survived with kneecaps intact, by the way.)

• What sort of things do people talk about? Successes? Failures? Customers? Sports? Other people?!

What's the general 'chat' in the office, or out on the road? The football game at the weekend? The books that people are reading at the moment? The latest Netflix series? Again, look for patterns – there might not be a right or wrong here, but it is indicative of the informal culture of your business.

What aspects of your business do people talk about, and how? Are they (like the rather extreme example above) rude and dismissive about customers behind their backs? If so, then whatever you might claim, you don't have a culture of putting customers first. Is there office tittle-tattle and malicious gossip about team members? Then whatever you might think, you don't have a culture of teamwork and trust.

On the other hand, do people check in with colleagues to see if they need help, or how their projects are progressing? Do they speak of customers as though they actually like them?

Often it's HOW people talk about things that reveals the greatest amount about their culture and working paradigms.

Does the conversation revolve around numbers, people, tasks, challenges... or something else? Listen for patterns and think carefully about what this is telling you.

- What sort of language do they use? Formal? Informal? Academic? Jargon-filled? Is swearing acceptable?

Business jargon is the bane of my life, yet I'm aware that I'm not immune and will use vocabulary that doesn't mean much outside the sphere in which I work. What sort of language do people use, both verbally and in written communication? Are emails written in a "Hi Jim – following on from our phone call..." manner, or a "Dear Jim, further to our prior communications I am delighted to inform you..."? What's the 'voice' with which you as a business speak, and with which people speak to each other?

- What sort of routines do you have? Does everyone go out for a drink after work on a Friday? Do people bring in cakes on their birthday? Do people gather round the water cooler to have the REAL conversation when the meeting is over?

Everyday routines are also part of your culture, because they are just part of what you do day to day. When I've worked in Saudi Arabia, we will stop whatever we're doing at certain points in the day for my colleagues to go to prayers, as required by their faith. Some clients in the UK will need their workshops or strategy sessions to finish early in the day, because that's what their shift patterns are. Others will start the day with a stand up 'huddle' meeting or a 'toolbox talk' with their teams, to brief them for the day ahead.

It's their 'normal'.

There are informal routines too: everyone gets a card from the CEO on their birthday, someone brings in cakes on a Friday, people habitually use recycling bins rather than throwing everything out for landfill.

When I was head of marketing at the Royal Scottish Academy of Music and Drama (now the Royal Conservatoire of Scotland), Katie, one of my team members, bought a ceramic duck for the office(for reasons known only to her, I have to say – I think she'd just seen it in a shop window and taken a fancy to it). It stood atop a filing cabinet, and one summer's day, in an idle moment, another team member and I took it down quietly, cut up a piece of paper and 'dressed' it in a bikini and sunglasses, with a suitcase under its wing.

We quietly put the duck back and waited until someone noticed, which they did a while later, with some hilarity.

From then on, just from time to time, the duck would disappear and re-appear again dressed in something else – a Santa outfit at Christmas, a witch's hat for Halloween, and so on. It wasn't part of the overall business culture, but it was part of the culture of our team, and became part of an informal 'routine'.

Look beyond the obvious, and you'll see signs of your own culture that you've not noticed before. What are they telling you?

- Where are the informal power bases in your company? Who tends to rule the mood? What mood IS that?

I was working with an engineering company a few years ago, where there seemed to be, in the eyes of the directors, a bit of a 'cultural problem'. Upon investigation and following conversations with various people at different levels within the business, it appeared that although the senior managers were the nominal leaders of the organisation, there were others at a more functional level who were ruling the roost. In short, there was the formal organisational structure, and an informal, unspoken one where the actual day-to-day leaders were strong characters who had asserted their influence (and in some cases, were undermining what the leadership wanted to do).

In a past career I worked at the BBC, initially as hospitality co-ordinator, looking after guests (many of them famous!) on a live daily daytime TV show. There was, of course, an obvious hierarchy of producers, directors, floor managers and assistants, researchers and so on. However, there was a cleaner called Muriel who was the only person to go to if you really wanted to know what was going on in the building. Well past retirement age, sporting a dyed beehive hairdo with a little bow at the front, Muriel spoke in a strong local accent and had been there for years. And she knew EVERYTHING.

The point I'm making here is this: you'll have a formal hierarchy, based on your management structure, and an informal hierarchy, based around whoever chooses to put themselves (or who finds themselves by the will of others), at the top.

This really needs to be acknowledged more than it usually is: if the formal leadership in any way is seen as NOT leading in a given area, the informal leadership will take over.

Obviously enough, these informal networks can be leveraged. They can also be dangerous to your business if they go unchecked.

The questions above are perhaps highlighting areas where your company culture can most readily be seen. Some slightly more oblique ones, which may tease out further factors are:

- What is your office space like? Tidy? Cluttered? Colourful? Austere? To what extent does it reflect who you are as a business?

Your office environment is a reflection of, and will have an impact on, your business culture. Do you think of yourselves as being in a fun, vibrant place to work, but your walls are battleship grey with little in the way of colourful visuals? Is 'teamwork' a thing for you, but everyone works in little rabbit-hutch-style booths?

Sometimes the nature of your work will dictate your environment. A biotech laboratory will have to be clinical and immaculate. A manufacturing plant will clearly be technical and functional above all else. But what about communal staff areas? Do you have (as I've seen in many companies) warm and well-furnished kitchen and social areas – in one case with a pool table where lunchtime competitions took place? Or is it a draughty hellhole with stained carpet, a sink and a microwave, and plastic chairs that are too uncomfortable to sit on for more than five minutes at a stretch?

In exactly the same way that you can walk into someone's home and tell a lot about them by the decor, people can walk into your business and identify core elements of your culture.

- What are the symbols of authority? A corner office, perhaps? Awards and certificates on the wall? A fancy desk or a seat by the window?

As a student, I had a summer job making light switches in a local factory. We had to clock in and clock out at the start and finish of our shifts, and we had set break times in the morning and afternoon. If we wanted a drink at any other time, we'd have to go downstairs to the staffroom and get a cup of something from the vending machine, which was one of those ones which dispensed incredibly thin plastic cups, and filled them with boiling liquid right to the very top, making their transportation back upstairs a tricky endeavour.

One of the team leaders, though, had a piece of plastic with six slightly smaller than cup-sized holes in it, enabling her to carry half a dozen cups up the stairs at a time.

On one occasion I was heading downstairs for a cup of tea, and offered to get some for the colleagues who were sitting round me. I approached the team leader and asked if I could borrow her tray.

In all seriousness, she turned to me and refused, on the basis that this was 'a team leader tray'. So we all had to make individual trips down to the vending machine.

Yes, it sounds ridiculous, but again it points to a pattern in unconscious human behaviour: people will create a hierarchy using whatever is at their disposal, and the most unlikely objects can become 'symbols' of something.

More obvious examples might include a named parking space near the door, a private office or a nice company car. Look closely within your own business – where are the trappings of power, both formal and informal?

- Remember the Big Five? If your business was a person, where would they be on each of the Big Five personality profile scales?

"THE BIG FIVE"

OPENNESS TO EXPERIENCE

Stick to what we know   Love the change!

CONSCIENTIOUSNESS

Disciplined and organised   Easygoing, spontaneous

EXTRAVERSION

Outgoing, energetic   Solitary, reserved

AGREEABLENESS

Friendly, approachable   Detached, challenging

NUEROTICISM

Sensitive, nervous   Secure, confident

Viewing your business as a person can give useful insights into your current culture and working paradigms. Again, you must be really honest – it's too easy with this sort of thing to put your mark on each spectrum where you'd like to think it is rather than where it actually is. Involving other people, sharing perspectives and looking for patterns is the way forward here, while bearing in mind that different functions within your business might have different sub-cultures that have formed around the main business culture.

- If your business was a celebrity, who would it be? Why?
- If your business was a plant, what would it be?
- If your business was a sandwich, what would it be?

These last three questions are ones I asked in a workshop for some drama students, years ago. I'd been asked by the Head of Acting to run a workshop to help his students promote a short play at the world-renowned Edinburgh Festival later that year.

Working in small groups, the students had chosen a short production, and I was trying to help them identify the overall feel or 'brand' of that production, so that they would be able to design their marketing materials accordingly. I mention this because external brand and internal culture are two sides of the same coin.

Two groups stick in my mind to this day. The first group had said openly from the outset that they were "theatre for the common man – no arty-farty nonsense." Their chosen celebrity was Bob Hoskins, their plant was grass, and their sandwich was plain old cheese and chutney.

Another group were working on a production that was somewhat different in nature – dark and dangerous. Their celebrity was Gary Oldman as Dracula, their sandwich was one of rare roast beef, with the blood seeping into the bread... and their plant? Any guesses? (I'll tell you at the end of the section.)

One of the things that you might find as you delve into your company culture as it stands at the moment is that there are variations according to department or function. This in itself isn't surprising: the way in which the IT team works isn't going to be the same as the way in which the marketing team or the finance team work.

The thing to look out for here is this: where are the points of commonality across all departments – this is who we are – and where are the differences that form sub-cultures?

The follow-on question from this, moving forward, is what are the core paradigms of your business, common across the entire organisation? Where are there allowable sub-cultures? And where might departments or functions develop into something that ceases to be helpful and puts them at odds with the rest of the business?

Oh – and that plant the second group of students had chosen? Venus flytrap. But you guessed that, didn't you?

Your future culture

Once you know where you are, it's time to define where you want to go.

This isn't about an "off with the old, on with the new" approach where you might lose some of the positive aspects of your current culture. It's about knowing what you want to take with you and what you want to leave behind: the whole-business equivalent, as it were, of 'learn, leverage or leave'. What is your core culture that will be the same no matter where you are in the world or how big the business gets... and what are the allowable sub-cultures that will inevitably develop in different parts of the business?

Our starting points here are twofold: your strategy and your business values.

- Will the current culture you've described provide the right environment to support your ambitious future plans?

- Does your current culture mirror the values that you hold personally and those that you've said your business holds?

- What aspects of your current culture are valuable, which you want to take forward into the future? What must be left behind?

Crucially... what do you have to DO to make it happen?

CHAPTER SUMMARY:

- Your culture is what it is...not what you say it is.
- Have a clear idea of what your cultural paradigms are, and what you want them to be.
- Your internal culture and your external brand are two sides of the same coin.

NOTES:

CHAPTER 13

CONSCIOUSLY CREATING YOUR CULTURE

Businesses are increasingly realising how important culture truly is in terms of their bottom line, and in terms of actually getting things done. Whilst there's plenty of talk about what needs to be done, there's far less talk about how.

The truth is once you've decided what you want your culture to be, there are practical steps you can – and indeed must – take to ensure that it happens.

Processes and systems

Funnily enough, the very area of your business that seems most removed from the 'people side' is one that can be the making of it, or, at the other end of the scale, one that can undermine it completely.

Looking back at your existing processes and systems, and the ones you'll need moving forward, are they supporting or undermining what you want to see in your future culture?

By way of example, a customer database which enables you to capture personal information as well as business data–one that, for instance, facilitates reminders about birthdays or recent family holidays – would tie in with a culture of being customer-focused.

An example of where processes were actually undermining company values and bringing about an unhealthy culture came to light a few years ago in the automotive industry. Whilst a particular well-known car mechanic promoted themselves on the basis of customer care and high standards of service, their sales processes involved staff earning bonuses based on...you guessed it...the volume of sales they brought in.

Perhaps unsurprisingly, this led to a tendency of staff to oversell products and services that might not have been necessary to the customer, in order to make their own bonuses. In some cases, staff were claiming that they had replaced a part when they'd done nothing of the sort, because it didn't need doing in the first place.

Once this was discovered and highlighted in a series of undercover TV consumer programmes, brand damage was done.

Look closely at your processes. If they were followed to the letter, what sort of behaviours would they be driving, and are these in line with your company values – what you actually want your working paradigms to be and how you want your staff to behave?

Performance measures

If you've spotted a gap where your processes (or the requirement to follow them) may not be contributing to the culture you want, you'll need to address it, and this can involve finding a balance between people following the process, yet not becoming slaves to the process to the extent that they stop thinking for themselves or acting with integrity.

This often involves bringing your business values and strategy into play when you review and measure performance. You're measuring sales figures, but you're also measuring the manner in which those sales were transacted.

Let's imagine that your business values include teamwork and customer focus, and your current strategy is focused on business growth and innovation. What might these things look like in real life, and how might you translate these broad concepts into clearly defined, measurable actions that can be demonstrated and proven? How might these actions differ depending on the leadership level of the person being reviewed?

Corporates refer to it as a competency framework, but I prefer something more down to Earth, like 'guiding principles'. Something based on the values mentioned above might look like this:

	TEAMWORK	CUSTOMER FOCUS	GROWTH	INNOVATION
Team member	I understand the business objectives of my my team and how I contribute to them	I go beyond basic requirements to serve my customers	I look for opportunities for business growth	I identify innovative approaches within my role
	I communicate openly and build trust with my colleagues	I look for opportunities to improve the customer experience	I am aware of my personal impact on business results	I take personal accountability for improvement in my business area
	I am aware of colleagues' work in the wider business and how my work impacts on it		I respond practically and positively to change	I add value to the business
Manager	As above, plus...	As above, plus...	As above, plus...	As above, plus...
	I clearly communicate business goals to my team	I maintain a clear line-of-sight between our customers and the day to day work of my team	I ensure my team is aware of the growth strategy and our role in it	I actively encourage new ideas
	I build collaborative partnerships cross-functionally to achieve business goals	I balance business and functional requirements with customer needs	I adapt to changing business demands and bring my team with me	I set high standards of excellence and hold my team to accounts

This is just an outline example – you'd probably want to include three or four factors under each heading, and then consider how someone would actually behave if they were working to these principles. If they've met their sales target, but stabbed everyone else in the back to get there, is that 'teamwork', and does it build a positive culture? In the short term, it might not look as though it matters if they are bringing in the money, but think carefully about the longer-term impact: low team morale, mistrust, lost productivity and the loss of good staff.

I was once in a meeting where a senior manager openly said that as long as her department was making the numbers, who cared? It soon became clear that people in her team were stressed, taking time off work, and some were actively looking to transfer out of her team. She may have been gaining on the swings, but she was losing on the roundabouts, and invisibly haemorrhaging money and goodwill in the process.

As you actively develop your working paradigms and create a culture that encourages your people to deliver on your strategy and broader aspirations, make sure you have an idea of the sort of indicators you'll look out for – things that will tell you whether you're on the right track. Happy, proactive staff, high motivation levels and client retention would be three obvious indicators – what are yours?

Your physical environment

It should come as no surprise that the physical environment in which we find ourselves has an impact on how we perform. I remember a documentary a few years ago where a head teacher had been drafted into an inner-city school that had major problems with non-attendance and low achievement. As one of his reform measures, he set about making the school a more pleasant place to be, changing the locker layouts to be more open (therefore reducing thefts) and brightening up the decor.

One of the day-to-day occurrences in the past had been scuffles between pupils as they were moving along the corridors between classes, and no one would step aside for anyone else. His solution was to put 'road markings' on the floor, so pupils walking in one direction were on one side of the dotted line, and pupils heading the other way were on the other side. Fights between classes were reduced significantly.

Think about some of the office environments you've worked in. At a basic level, is it a nice place to be? Or a poorly heated, featureless box with paint peeling off the walls?

One of the worst training rooms I've ever found myself in was the offices of a large government organisation. There was an uneven table in the middle of the room, and several of the chairs were stained or had fabric fraying at the edges. Someone had left a cup of tea on the side, and it had been sitting around for so long that a disc of mould had grown on the top. There were broken tables piled up in one corner of the room, and although this client had asked for an on-screen presentation to accompany the workshop, there was no projection screen, just a couple of pieces of flip chart paper stuck to the grubby wall. (I never worked with them again.)

Not only was it a depressing scene for anyone who walked in, but it conveyed, in its way, the company's culture towards learning: it didn't matter. It was an afterthought; it wasn't really worth much effort or expenditure. These were underlying messages that everyone who entered the room would have picked up.

Obviously, I'm not suggesting that everyone goes out and hires a costly interior designer or splashes out on expensive furniture, but pay the working environment some attention. It makes a difference.

Another frequently overlooked 'physical' aspect of your workplace paradigm is what people wear. Having worked with many different businesses in a range of sectors over the years, this becomes very obvious. Everyone at Avon Cosmetics seemed to be a fashion icon, beautifully dressed and made up. Sometimes I felt the pressure of having to ramp up my game and accessorise and co-ordinate in order to keep up!

Major banks like RBS or HSBC were a different matter altogether – formal professional was the order of the day, and if I wore anything less than a suit or a businesslike dress, I'd feel as though I didn't look up to the mark.

Other smaller companies also have had their own style: some relaxed and informal, with staff coming in in jeans, and others displaying their creative flair with bright hair colours and loud fashions.

How does this very visible aspect of your workplace reflect its culture? Is it in line with the culture you want to have, moving forward?

Culture vs. brand

Some of what I've said here might be more readily associated with your brand than your internal working paradigms and culture, but in truth they are two sides of the same coin.

If there's a mismatch between culture and brand, your team will believe the internal culture, and the discrepancy between what actually happens day by day, and what you might be telling people externally, is bound to surface at some point, to your detriment.

What are your brand values, and how do they show up in your day-to-day culture? Where might you be better able to align the two?

Leadership

Here, friends, is where we come full circle. One of the key drivers of any business culture is the behaviour or leadership style of those at the top. Without exception, people further down the organisation will follow what the leaders do far more than they will do what they say.

A company I worked with once wanted to introduce more of a coaching culture into the business (following the Sir John Whitmore model), and so was putting all its middle managers through a coaching course. As part of this, the senior leadership team were coming in to speak to the different groups to share their experiences.

On one occasion, I was briefing one of the leadership team members, suggesting that it would be a good idea for him to outline how he uses coaching with his own team, and how the directors use the technique between themselves.

"Oh, I don't really have time for it myself", he said breezily. In which case, it was never going to happen. Why would anyone else bother to learn and implement new skills if the leaders weren't going to?

If leaders don't role model, champion and drive the cultural paradigms that they want to see, it won't happen. Someone or something else will dictate the pace.

Look closely at the paradigms your business will need in the coming years to support your vision, purpose and strategy.

What are you and your leadership team currently doing to role model this, and what do you need to change in order to lead by example? How will you keep each other on track, and hold one another to account?

Coming full circle back to our work in 'Pea #1: Personal', what is the leadership character and legacy that you want to leave?

Who do you and your leadership team need to become in order to build a culture that helps your people to deliver on your strategy, and on your own personal goals and aspirations?

As long as YOU keep growing, your business will, too.

CHAPTER SUMMARY:

- Ensure that your frameworks and processes support the behaviours and culture you are driving towards.

- Externalise your culture: create a physical environment that reflects the cultural paradigms that you want.

- Culture and brand must be aligned, or your team will lose faith in your brand.

- As a leader, role model and champion what you want to see in your own culture.

NOTES:

AND FINALLY...

And there we have it – The 5 Peas Framework™:

Personal. Purpose. People. Process. Paradigms.

Five core principles that, as you grow your business, might otherwise be forgotten or overlooked while you focus on the engine room of generating revenue.

Never lose sight of your own **Personal** growth, not just because it's important for your business, but because it's important to YOU as a person.

Stay true to your **Purpose**: your vision, mission, values and strategy. They will be, as JRR Tolkien put it in *Lord of the Rings*, your "light in the darkness, when all other lights go out."

Look after your **People** – your business depends on how they deliver for you. We are all human: we are unique, and yet we are all the same.

Remember that a **Process** doesn't exist on its own – it's designed, driven, managed and improved by people. Manage your processes – don't let them manage you.

Carefully create your cultural **Paradigms** so that your business and everyone in it and associated with it thrives, rather than merely survives.

Life and business can be tricky enough – make sure you travel the journey well.

Warmest regards,

Annabelle

REFERENCES

PSI Basic and PSI7 programmes run by PSI Seminars, Clearlake Oaks, CA. www.psiseminars.com

Ofman, D. (2001). *Core qualities.* Schiedam: Scriptum.

Senge, P. (1990). *The Fifth Discipline.* London: Random House.
(Using the Ladder of Inference devised by psychologist Chris Argyris)

The VitalityTest by Nicholas Haines at www.fiveinstitute.com

Goldberg, L.R. (2016).An alternative "Description of personality": The Big-Five factor structure. *Journal of Personality and Social Psychology* 59 (6).

Osterwalder, Pigneur et al *Business Model Generation: a handbook for visionaries, game changers and challengers.* 2010

Goleman, D. (1995). *Working with Emotional Intelligence.*
London: Bloomsbury.

Corporate Culture: Evidence from the Field (2016).
Columbia Business School Research Paper No. 16-49.

Whitmore, J. (2009). *Coaching for Performance.*
London: Nicholas Brealey Publishing.

Iain Forrest Photography

ABOUT THE AUTHOR

Annabelle Beckwith has been a consultant, coach and trainer since the early 2000s, working with entrepreneurs, SMEs and global corporates in all sectors, and with clients all over the world.

She is the founder of Yara Journeys (at www.yara-journeys.com), a consultancy specialising in leadership development, working with business owners and executives to develop themselves personally, as well as building the strategic and practical abilities they need for success.

Annabelle has been quoted in various publications, including Arianna Huffington's *Thrive Global*, *Entrepreneur* and *Forbes* online, and has authored online books including *Goal Setting for Success*, at bookboon.com, and *A Quick Guide to Indian Culture*.

She is frequently in demand as a speaker, presenting her down-to-Earth, no-nonsense approach with humour and compassion, and focusing on life and business journeys as well as achieving aspirations and reaching strategic goals.

Annabelle lives by the sea in Ayrshire, Scotland with her two children.

Her personal website is at www.annabellebeckwith.com.

For free downloads and templates
related to
GET YOUR PEAS IN A ROW

please visit
www.annabellebeckwith.com/downloads

Giving a Voice to Creativity!

With every donation, a voice will be given to the creativity that lies within the hearts of our children living with diverse challenges.

By making this difference, children that may not have been given the opportunity to have their Heart Heard will have the freedom to create beautiful works of art and musical creations.

Donate by visiting

HeartstobeHeard.com

We thank you.